This book is
the last

The New Manual of
Public Speaking

The New Manual of Public Speaking

Edited by Derek Hall

W. Foulsham & Co. Ltd.
London · New York · Toronto · Cape Town · Sydney

W. Foulsham & Company Limited
Yeovil Road, Slough, Berkshire, SL1 4JH

ISBN 0–572–01365–5

Copyright © 1986 W. Foulsham & Co. Ltd.

Printed in Great Britain by St Edmundsbury Press,
Bury St Edmunds, Suffolk

Contents

1. Introduction

Why speak in public?

There are many reasons why you may have to speak in public. Perhaps in your job you have to present a report of a project or contribute a talk at a conference. As the head of a firm you may be the obvious person to give a speech at an employee's leaving presentation, or you may have to speak on behalf of your company in a radio or television interview. Your hobby, too, may involve you in chairing a meeting of a society to which you belong, or you may be asked to give a talk on the hobby to another group. Your social life may also lead to various public speaking engagements, from proposing a short toast at a wedding to giving an after-dinner speech. How to perform well at all these types of public speaking, and many others besides, are covered in this book which aims to provide guidance to people new to public speaking as well as giving some useful hints to those with rather more experience.

Is it possible to learn public speaking?

Some people seem to have a natural gift for public speaking, but many of us, at least to begin with, face such a prospect with a certain amount of fear and trepidation. You can take some comfort, however, from the fact that people who have tried to analyse what makes a successful and effective speech suggest that about 90 per cent is dependent on having something worthwhile to say and putting it over well (which can be learnt) and only about 10 per cent depends on your personality (which you cannot easily change). Therefore, most people can learn to give an adequate and enjoyable speech, even if they may never be great orators.

As with most other skills, there are no short cuts to learning about public speaking. You should not, therefore, expect instant confidence when addressing all and sundry. If you cast your mind back to other skills you may have mastered earlier in your life, such as cycling or swimming, it was probably some time before you really felt confident at them. You will also almost certainly make mistakes, and some of these will be made in front of an audience. However, if you have the will to succeed at public speaking you should regard any such mistakes as useful experience – not to be repeated, you hope. The fact that many of the skills of public speaking are also good conversational skills, useful in your everyday life, can provide additional motivation.

How to learn the skills of public speaking

On the whole, children at school are taught far more about how to express themselves by the written word than in speech, and therefore most of us only really learn about public speaking when adult. You can learn a reasonable amount from reading books such as this, or attending courses in public speaking. However, much of what you learn will come from listening carefully to other speakers, and analysing what works and why. If you have an opportunity to watch a video of yourself speaking, you can analyse your performance in the same way.

You must, then, put what you are learning into practice; starting with short and reasonably easy types of public speaking and building up as your skills and confidence grow. You could, for example, offer to thank a speaker or propose a short toast, or even just start by contributing a few words to a discussion group or asking a question after a meeting. Next time you will probably find you are confident enough to talk a little more.

What makes a successful speech or talk?

As suggested earlier, your own personality may play only a small part in the success, or otherwise, of a speech. Having said that, it is a vital part, however, adding spice and individuality to what you say. You should always try to be sincere, only saying what you really believe. Audiences are quickly aware of insincerity and will respect you more for saying what you feel, even if they disagree with you, than for saying something false. You should, of course, write your own speeches, as it is difficult to give a speech written by someone else convincingly. Public speaking is different from acting, and you should not pretend to be someone different.

Adequate preparation and good presentation are also vital to success, and these topics are dealt with at some length later in this book. Probably the other most vital factor is having a good subject about which to talk, and an overall purpose to your speaking. In general terms, all public speaking serves one purpose – the communication of your ideas to a group of other people. However, this purpose can be broken down into a number of more specific aims and, although most types of speaking fulfil more than one of these aims, there is usually one of overriding importance. You should always be aware of this aim, as you are unlikely to be successful if you have not fully decided why you are speaking. In many talks and lectures the main aim is to inform or teach. Social speaking, such as after-dinner speeches, is usually more for entertainment, whereas in speaking to public meetings you are probably trying to persuade people or perhaps attempting to stimulate them into action.

How this book is arranged

As there are so many different types of public speaking it is impossible to treat them all together. The remainder of this book is therefore divided into four main parts. Chapter 2 deals with a few general subjects, such as increasing your background general knowledge and vocabulary. It also suggests ways in which you can make the best use of your voice. These are things which will help you in general conversation as well as in public speaking, and which you can think about and improve at any time rather than when you have a specific public speaking engagement in mind.

Chapters 3 to 5 deal with the practicalities of speaking before a live audience. A large part of this (Chapter 3) deals with preparation, using the example of a reasonably long talk in front of a group of strangers. It may be worth explaining here the reasoning behind the 'note card' method suggested, as other methods are sometimes advocated. Experienced speakers may feel that notes of any kind are unnecessary, and that you should just think about what you are going to say, then get up and say it. This may work for them, and will certainly sound spontaneous, but an inexperienced speaker is more likely to stand up and then find his mind has gone blank! Other people may suggest that you should read from full notes or should memorise your speech word for word. These methods both have problems. Audiences tend to dislike being read to – after all they could have read the speech themselves in the comfort of their own homes. You also run the risk of situations such as that encountered by one speaker who read 'I am agreeably surprised . . .', then, as he finally succeeded in turning to the next page, '. . . to find such a large and dignified audience here tonight'. The large and dignified audience burst into laughter. Memorising your speech gives you the additional strain of trying to remember what comes next, and you are also easily thrown by unexpected circumstances. This is why the method of using note cards as guidelines to keep you roughly to your planned speech, while allowing a certain amount of flexibility, is advocated here. With note cards you can expand and contract what you say as necessary, and you are also able to respond to the audience and their reactions. You are also less likely to panic and suffer from a blank mind than if you try to speak 'off the cuff', as you are given confidence by the fact that you have the cards to remind you of what to say next.

Chapter 4 deals with the practicalities of public speaking once you are at the venue. It also covers events that may happen during your talk that cannot be planned for in advance. Chapter 5 deals with the special features of other types of public speaking before a live audience, relating them to the aspects dealt with in more detail in Chapters 3 and 4. At the end of the book, sample speeches are given for some of the types, but it should be stressed that these are for guidance only. A successful speech must be one that you have written and planned yourself.

Speaking on television and radio are dealt with in Chapter 6. There are several similarities to talking before a live audience, but several important differences as well.

Finally, Chapters 7 and 8 deal with controlling and contributing to meetings and other events. A chairman's duties (Chapter 7) involve him in public speaking, but of a different kind from that described in the other chapters. Instead of presenting a prepared speech, a chairman's job is primarily to make sure that an event is conducted satisfactorily. Most of his speaking will have to be done extemporaneously, responding to any situation as it arises. Chairmen, therefore, need to be well versed in the formalities of meetings and committees, and some of the main features of these are dealt with in Chapter 8.

Two other points should be made about this book. Firstly, for the sake of brevity, male words such as 'he' or 'chairman' are used throughout the book. Women can be just as successful at public speaking as men, and the words 'he' and 'chairman' should therefore be taken to mean persons of either sex. Secondly, like any other 'rules', the suggestions made here can be ignored by some people with success. You should remember that they are only guidelines, designed to help most of the people most of the time.

2. Building Up Your Confidence

Coping with nervousness

If you are nervous at the thought of speaking in public, you can take comfort from the fact that you are by no means alone. There are many examples of great and well-known speakers who have managed to overcome their initial fears, and even additional handicaps such as a pronounced stammer. Another great confidence booster is the thought that most of your audience would be much more nervous than you – they probably admire the fact that you are brave enough to undertake public speaking and wish that they had your degree of confidence!

A certain amount of nervousness is, in fact, necessary for successful public speaking. Speakers who are very self-confident are often not particularly alert to the reactions and needs of the audience. They also tend to make mistakes because they are not prepared to learn. So, although you obviously will need to overcome the worst of your fears, a certain amount of nervousness is a positive asset.

In discussing nervousness about public speaking, it is useful to look at the different types of fears people may have. Many of them are quite trivial when analysed logically (though it is not always easy to convince yourself!), or can be dealt with by thorough preparation to minimise the chances of a dreaded situation occurring.

Fear of the unknown Hopefully, this book will give you some idea of what to expect from public speaking. If you follow the suggestions concerning preparation, and enquiring about the likely audience, venue and programme, you should know roughly what to expect. Obviously, as you become more experienced in public speaking you will gain more confidence about coping with all situations.

Fear of making a fool of yourself   Most people imagine they have far more faults than are noticed by others. Even if you say or do something silly it will not be the end of the world, and audiences do realise that you are only human, too. If you are well prepared and rehearsed, and then concentrate on what you are saying during your speech, you will minimise the chances of something going wrong.

Fear of losing the attention or support of the audience Most audiences are there because they are interested in what you have to say, and usually they want you to succeed in your speech. The cards are therefore stacked in your favour. If you attempt to tune in to your audience, as you would in a normal conversation with a friend, you will be able to respond to them well and there is no reason why you should not succeed.

Fear of being misunderstood   Again, the likelihood of this occurring can be minimised by being well prepared and rehearsed. If you know your subject well, and have planned a logical treatment, you should have few fears in this direction.

Fear of being inaudible   If you practise using your voice well, as detailed later in this chapter, you should have no problems with audibility.

Fear of losing your place in your talk and/or drying up   If, as suggested, you use note cards as prompts for your talk, you should not have too much difficulty in following where you are. Don't worry about pauses as you glance down at the card for your next point – such pauses will help to structure the talk and make it easier for the audience to follow.

Fear of the physical reactions to nervousness   You probably feel only too familiar with the manifestations of nervousness, such as weak and wobbly knees, shaking hands, a dry mouth, a constricted feeling in the chest and a mind which seems unable to think clearly. It is possible to minimise if not eliminate these reactions, and hints on how to do this are given in Chapter 4.

Increasing your general knowledge and vocabulary

In addition to a thorough knowledge of any specialised subject on which he is talking it also is useful if a speaker has a broad background of general knowledge. A good public speaker also needs to have a genuine interest in people and words.

A wide general knowledge will enable you to include interesting facts and ideas, whatever the subject of your speech. In order to acquire this knowledge you need to be observant and to develop a system for storing material which you think may be useful or which particularly appeals to you. You will no doubt remember some facts, but many public speakers find it useful to have a notebook handy, in which they can note odd ideas or facts before they get forgotten. Cuttings from newspapers and magazines can also be very useful sources of information and ideas. How you file these will depend on your personal inclinations, but one of the most important things to remember is that information is of no use unless you are able to retrieve it.

Many people use keywords to identify the main subject area, and file the notes or cuttings within a loose-leaf or card index system which retains a fair amount of flexibility to meet their changing needs. Always note the source and date on any notes or cuttings. Then when you come to use the information, you will know how reliable and up-to-date it is likely to be. You will probably also find that you need to undertake a periodic thinning to prevent the system getting clogged up with old and redundant material. If you have time you may do best to precis a whole mass of information by writing your own notes. As well as helping you to remember the facts, this will also provide valuable experience in putting material into your own words in a concise form – always useful in public speaking!

As well as collecting notes and cuttings, you may also find it useful to develop your mental agility. Try to analyse why you like something – perhaps a favourite book or television programme. Also, practise thinking about everyday subjects from all angles, as this will help you when you are trying to think about the various treatments possible for the subject of your speech.

An interest in people will help you deal with different kinds of audiences – perhaps ones with a completely different background to yourself – and to react to the audience as you discover how they respond.

Wide and voracious reading will help develop your vocabulary. Good public speakers need a wide vocabulary, not to 'impress' their audiences with long words, but so that they can choose the most apt and interesting word in any situation. Thesauri and dictionaries are useful both to remind you of old alternatives you had perhaps forgotten and to suggest and define new words. If you find a new word that particularly appeals, use it in your ordinary conversation first before trying it out in a speech, and do make sure that its meaning will be clear to your audience and that you use it correctly. Even with commonly used words make sure that you are sure of the correct meanings – there are a number of pairs or groups of easily confused words. Always remember, however, that the best word is often the shortest and most commonly understood. You will only bore or irritate your audience with too many complex or unfamiliar words.

Using your voice

Regional accents and dialects are no longer regarded as a handicap to good speaking and do not need to be eliminated* but there are still ways in which most people can improve the clarity of what they say. However, any attempts to alter your voice presentation should not be attempted shortly before your speech. If you actively attempt to improve your articulation, pronunciation, etc., in normal conversation you should then automatically do so in your public speaking. As well as dealing with any particular voice problems you may have, you can help yourself in general by using your voice and ears fully. Read aloud as much as possible – anything from telling your children stories to reading out the examples of the speeches in this book. Use your ears to listen carefully to other people's voices, both when they are well and when they are poorly used, and analyse what you hear.

---

*However, if you are speaking beyond your local area you should speak a little more slowly and avoid or explain local dialect words.

Some people speak in a rather slovenly fashion, failing to articulate all their words fully. 'Is he', for example, ends up as 'izzee', and 'got to' as 'gorra'. If this is a problem you are probably not opening your mouth sufficiently. It may help deliberately to try to form words on the tip of your tongue against your front teeth. Saying 'tongue twisters' without slurring the words together is also good practice.

Another common example of poor pronunciation is the dropping of consonants. 'Beaten' then becomes 'bea'en'. Consonants – in particular 'r's – may also get added where they are not needed. For example 'idea' may end up as 'idear'. In both cases all you can do is to try to pronounce your words more clearly and correctly in normal conversation so that you automatically do so in your speeches. Dictionaries and pronunciation guides can help if you are unsure of the generally accepted pronunciation of words, but do remember that it is more important that your words should be clear to all listeners than that you 'correctly' pronounce 'controversy' or similar words.

Some people are prone to gabble through their sentences both in ordinary conversation and in public speaking. To be clearly understood speaking in public, you should deliberately aim to speak slightly more slowly than usual – though not funereally. However, all your speech should not be at the same speed. If you are making a solemn or important point you should tend to speak slowly, while parts of the speech in a lighter vein are more appropriately spoken slightly more quickly.

Changes in tone, likewise, help to structure a speech. If you actually think about, and react to, what you are saying you should find that your emotions naturally lead to an appropriate tone and pace. A flat and expressionless voice usually means that your voice and brain are not working in harmony – and that you are not really interested in what you are saying. This may happen because you are expressing someone else's words or ideas, or perhaps because you have tried to memorise too much of your speech and all your concentration is going into trying to remember words. Be particularly careful not to let the ends of your sentences just fade away. This sometimes happens because you are jumping ahead and thinking about what you will say next, rather than concentrating on the sentence being spoken.

Another result of your voice and brain being out of harmony, perhaps because of distractions, may be a tendency to hesitate unduly. As stressed throughout the book short, quiet pauses actually help to structure a speech, but longer pauses, or pauses filled with gibberish or muttering, are irritating to the audience. If you are prone to these problems you must concentrate fully on what you are saying. You may also find it helps to make your note cards slightly longer than suggested in later chapters. Include on them most of the names and technical terms you will use as these tend to be particularly easy to forget, thus causing hesitation.

The pitch of your voice is something you cannot change, and it is inadvisable to try to lower the pitch of a high voice. You will almost certainly lapse back to your natural pitch if you lose your concentration, and this will be more distracting than a high pitch throughout.

Finally, volume. Do remember that a loud voice will not compensate for poor articulation. With the help of a friend, practise throwing your voice different distances so that when you are faced with an unknown hall in which to speak you will know roughly the volume that is needed. The voice level tends to follow the eyes, so if you look to the back of the hall your voice will probably be at about the right level. Looking towards the distance you want your voice to carry will also help to ensure that you hold your head up, rather than mumbling down towards your feet or note cards.

Gestures and mannerisms

When you are giving a speech or talk, your body as well as your voice is communicating with your audience. If this sounds improbable, try watching a television programme with the sound turned down – you may be surprised how much you can gather just from the way the people move. Gestures and mannerisms can both add to and detract from a talk. If the movements are unrelated to what you are saying – for example a nervous twiddling of a pencil or a tendency to shrug the shoulders at frequent intervals – they will be distracting. You should try to eliminate such habits as far as possible. However, gestures appropriate to what you are saying can help reinforce the verbal message. Sharp, strong gestures are appropriate to rousing calls to action or when you are expressing your indignation, whereas quiet, contemplative words should be accompanied by limited movement and only gentle gestures. The type and quantity of gestures used during a speech should also be linked to your personal style and the size of the audience. In a small room, any kind of exaggerated gesture would probably seem out of place, whereas a weak gesture in front of a large audience would look ineffectual. However, whatever the size of the audience don't overdo the gestures.

As with the tone of your voice, you should try, as far as possible, to let your emotions naturally guide your gestures. However, by watching others and by watching yourself in a mirror you will get an idea of how to use movements as a positive asset rather than a distraction.

Knowing the correct form of address

Although most meetings nowadays are rather less formally conducted than in the past, you will still be expected to start most talks and speeches with a formal address. Although it may sometimes seem over-grand, the formal address is a help to both you and the audience. It is an easy to remember and ritualised way for you to get started – always the worst part of public speaking – and it also gives the audience a chance to 'tune in' to your voice before you say anything particularly important. In many cases a straightforward 'Mr Chairman, Ladies and Gentlemen' will suffice, but if you are addressing special guests and/or titled persons the rules get rather more complicated. There is not space to deal with all possibilities here, but you may be able to get advice from the organiser of the event. Your local library will almost certainly have a number of books which deal with the formal rules of protocol.

In nearly all cases you should start a formal address by addressing the chair; the only exception is if royalty is present. 'Mr (or Madam) Chairman' is the usual version, but forms such as 'Mr President' or 'My Lord and President' may sometimes also be used.

You would then mention any special guests by name, and this is where most pitfalls are likely. This is followed by 'My Lords (and Ladies)' if there are any peers present who have not been mentioned as special guests. Finally, the rest of the audience is addressed by 'Ladies and Gentlemen'. With a single-sex audience just one of these should be used, of course, and in certain situations you may also choose to use some other appropriate form of address. For example, trade unionists often address their audience as 'Comrades', and if you are speaking to a group to which you belong you may address the audience as 'Fellow Members'.

3. Preparing a Talk

Public speaking resembles decorating, in that time and effort spent on thorough preparation is repaid by a better and more professional end result. Like the wallpaper and the top coat of paint, the speech itself is just the final surface, and it cannot be expected to go smoothly if it does not have a well-prepared base. You should not, therefore, try to make a speech without preparation; you may get away with it once or twice, but you will probably not be happy with the result, and will perhaps lose your confidence and keenness to continue speaking in public.

Much of the programme of preparation outlined in the remainder of this chapter, and the next chapter which deals with events once you reach the venue, applies to all types of public speaking in front of a live audience. However, rather than generalise too much, the chapters are biased towards a speaker giving a reasonably long talk to a group of strangers. It is assumed that the subject of the talk is something about which the speaker knows a reasonable amount, for example his hobby. There is also a section on the use of visual aids. A later chapter (Chapter 5) deals with points particularly relevant to other types of public speaking.

To some readers, especially those with some experience of public speaking, the programme of preparation suggested here may seem unnecessarily detailed. By all means ignore some of the suggestions. However, especially if you are a raw beginner, the more preparation you can do the more likely it is that everything will go smoothly on the day.

Obtaining details about the talk

You may be approached to give a talk anything from a year or more to a few weeks in advance. If you feel the time allowed is insufficient for proper preparation, it may be better to refuse the invitation altogether. If you are asked well in advance, do put the date on a calendar or diary so that you don't forget it! It may also be worthwhile adding a note to yourself a month or so ahead of the date as a reminder to start the main preparation, though obviously you can do much useful thinking and planning before that.

Before you agree to give a talk you will need to find out certain basic details. You can also plan your talk more easily if you ask for other information. If the talk is planned well in advance, you may not be able to get all the details immediately, but before you begin your main preparation you should have asked most of the questions listed below.

Basic details   when (date and time)

where (including which room if in a large building)

subject and title of talk*

length of talk required

type of talk required (e.g. illustrated)

fees or expenses available (if these are likely to affect your willingness to give the talk)

name and type of organisation or society asking you to talk

name and telephone number of the organiser.

Likely audience* size

age

sex

occupation(s) or interest(s) – will they all be members of the organising society and

---

*Covered in more detail in the following sections.

thus presumably share at least one interest, or will there be guests and other out-
siders too?

do they want to be educated or entertained, or a mixture of both?

how much do they already know about the
subject of the talk?

The programme* is yours the only talk?

if there are other speakers at the same
event: how many, who, what are they
speaking on, and what is the order of
speakers?

will there be refreshments, an interval or
society business – if so, when?

The venue* size and shape of room

will you be speaking from a platform?

what are the acoustics like?

will a microphone be provided – if so what
type?

if the talk is to be illustrated what equipment will be provided and what will you
need to bring – film or slide-projector,
screen, pointer?

will a projectionist or long-distance control
mechanism be available for any slide-
projector

are the blackout facilities adequate (especially if it is a day-time talk)?

if you intend to use a video will suitable
equipment be available?

(for electrical equipment) – is the electric-
ity supply the modern square 3-pin variety

and are there sufficient convenient sock-
ets?

is any other equipment you may need
available (e.g. blackboard, overhead projector, table, lectern, light for notes)?

if you intend to bring your own equipment
will there be a suitable place for it?

If preliminary arrangements are made by telephone, ask the
organiser to confirm in writing, at least the basic details such
as the date, time and place.

The subject and title of the talk

In many cases you will have been asked to speak on a
particular subject. If the choice is left up to you it is usually
best to talk on a subject which has roused your own enthusiasm. A subject that is in itself interesting – but not to
you – may not produce such a successful talk. Discuss and
agree the title with the organiser early on. You know the
subjects you intend to cover and should therefore, whenever possible, choose the title. However, the organiser may
be able to help with suggestions as to the kinds of titles that
seem to attract good turnouts to the meetings. Good titles
may be humorous, apt, punchy, provocative or topical, but
don't try to be too subtle; you don't want to hear afterwards
that people may have attended if only they had realised that
that was what you were going to speak about. You are also
more likely to keep your audience happy if the title gives
them some idea of the kind of talk to expect.

The audience

An audience is basically a group of people gathered
together. They may be strangers, but they react as a mass.
The reception you get depend on the majority of individual
reactions. Any information you have been able to obtain
about the likely audience can help you plan your talk. Large
audiences tend to act more as one mass than smaller ones,
and although it may be easier to generate enthusiasm or a
laugh, a larger audience is also more easily distracted. With

a large audience you need to be positive and emphatic; similar behaviour in front of a small group would appear too grandiose.

If your audience belongs to the same age group, it is usually safe to refer to events, dates or situations they would understand without elaborate explanations. Be careful though. Only people who were born before or during the Second World War will know exactly what it was like 'getting call-up papers' and similarly, only those born before the mid-1950s are likely to remember the 'winter of 1963' (when there was a long and widespread freeze-up in Britain).

Don't patronise or talk down to audiences of young or old people. A talk to children may sometimes require you to think of simpler words or explanations, and you may be able to think of points that will particularly appeal to them; however, they are not likely to thank you for talking to them in an inane 'kiddy'-type voice. Also remember that not all old people are deaf and/or feeble-minded. You should talk to them clearly, but there is no need to shout or to speak extremely slowly.

All the other questions about the audience suggested in the list may give you other useful pointers towards your approach. Do remember, though, that audiences can be unpredictable, so don't go to the talk with too many preconceived notions. As explained in the chapter on the talk itself (Chapter 4), both you and the audience will need to spend the first part of the talk adjusting to one another.

The programme

Even if you are the only speaker at a particular event, the group you are talking to may have other business to deal with and may want a break for refreshments at some stage. Many groups have a set order of proceedings, but if you have any influence on the arrangements it is best from the speaker's point of view if all business and domestic arrangements (including refreshments) are out of the way before you start your talk. This gives you the last word (except for the vote of thanks), and means that your talk is fresh in your audience's mind as they leave. It also prevents the embarrassments of either a sudden rush to put the kettle on as your talk ends, or the arrival of refreshments in the middle of question time. Neither will help the audience to concentrate on what you are saying.

Most talks tend to be followed by time for questions. You should discuss with the organiser early on whether there will indeed be a question time and if so how much time has been allowed for it. You may also wish to allow time to sum up the main points after question time, but this is probably more appropriate in the case of an educational talk or a speech exhorting the audience to do something, such as support a charity or vote for a certain candidate, than after a lighter 'entertainment' type talk.

If you are one of a number of speakers, you will have to keep in mind how your talk will relate to the others being given. If you are speaking late on in the programme keep in mind the fact that other speakers may overrun their allotted time and you may be asked to speak more briefly than originally agreed. However, less experienced speakers tend to be placed early on in the programme, leaving the 'star' speaker until last – in that case don't be the one who overruns and upsets the whole programme!

The venue

Prior knowledge about the venue and whether or not a microphone will be available, will help you to practice pitching your voice at a suitable level. The choice of whether or not to use a microphone is dealt with below. Knowledge about the venue and equipment available will also help you to decide what illustrations might be appropriate. Rooms and equipment can (and should) be inspected before the start of the talk so that you are not surprised by a much larger room than you expected, or by a non-functioning projector.

You may get no choice as to whether to use a microphone, and unless you are already familiar with the venue the organiser will probably have a better idea than you as to whether one is necessary. Although microphones may help your audibility they do have a number of disadvantages which should be considered. Firstly, are you happy about the idea of using a microphone? If you are nervous, the microphone will amplify any nervousness in your voice. A microphone is also prone to pick up other 'off stage' noises such as tapping, or a quiet aside. Alternatively, it may make its own squeaks and groans. Most microphones used for talks are of the fixed type and unless they are quite sophisticated and multidirectional you may have problems with fluctuating voice levels as you move your head. In any case the front rows may receive an irritating mixture of your natural and amplified voices. Finally, there are also the possibilities of knocking into the microphone or tripping over any wires.

Therefore, unless you think it is absolutely necessary, it is probably better not to use a microphone. Occasions where they are necessary include outside speaking, especially to a large crowd. Microphones are often also necessary when speaking in very long, 'cathedral-like' rooms (indeed in cathedrals themselves!). It is also very difficult for an audience to adjust quickly from amplified to normal voices, so if your talk is one of a series you would do best to 'join the crowd' if everyone else is using the microphone.

Initial thoughts

If you are given plenty of notice before your talk, there is little point in sitting down and trying to write it straightaway. If you've followed the suggestions in the previous chapter to improve your general knowledge and, assuming the subject is to do with your job or hobby, you should already have a good store of material for the talk. It is a good idea to keep a notebook or even a portable dictating machine handy and to note down any ideas, good phrases, illustrations, quotations, and facts which occur to you on the subject. Note them down in any order, and do not reject anything just because, at first, it seems unsuitable – later on it could turn out to be just the kind of idea you need or, if not, it may spark off other useful ideas. You may wish to ask colleagues or friends for ideas, but don't let them influence you too much or pour scorn on your own early efforts. Depending on your character, and the way you approach tasks, you may prefer to apply some concentrated thought to the subject instead of waiting for inspiration. In either case, try and dig deep into your mind so that you produce original thoughts and conclusions rather than just relying on superficial or second-hand material.

Preliminary planning

About three or four weeks before your talk you should aim to get down to finalising the main framework. This will probably only take an evening or so, but should be done well in advance to give you time to research any missing information. If you are to give an illustrated talk you may need to work out the general framework even earlier so that you can get hold of the relevant pictures or specimens.

Most talks can be divided into three main parts: the introduction or approach, the main body of the talk, and the conclusion. The introduction gives both you and your audience time to adjust to each other and allows you to explain how you propose to tackle the subject. A good introduction also enthuses and interests the audience and makes them eager for the rest of the talk. The conclusion gives you a chance to remind them of the main aspects of the subject and also a chance to spur them into action if your talk is intended to get the audience to do something. Both the introduction and conclusion are covered in more detail later in this chapter. In between comes the main body of the talk which is discussed below. To remind yourself of the basic breakdown, remember the often quoted maxim attributed to a sergeant major: 'First I tells 'em what I'm going to tell 'em, then I tells 'em, then I tells 'em what I've told 'em.'

When you tackle the preliminary planning, get out any notes you have made on the subject and, if possible, spend a little more time seeing if you can think of any other aspects which could perhaps be covered. Then sort your notes into related groupings. As you do this you may begin to see a pattern emerge and get some ideas for possible divisions of the main body of the talk. If you find you have large numbers of unrelated ideas you would probably do best to decide which two or three aspects you think are the most interesting, or best put over your argument. An audience is likely to be more impressed by a few, clearly expressed ideas than a whole mass of ideas loosely and illogically presented. Similarly, decide on two or three ideas to explore within each of these main divisions.

Write these subjects down as main headings and subheadings, and then see if you can arrange them in a logical way so that your talk will seem to have a natural flow. There are a number of ways in which subjects can be logically arranged, and you will obviously have to pick an approach which suits your subject matter. A chronological approach, going from the past, via the present, to the future, is a common treatment. Another successful approach may be to go from the familiar (an aspect to which your audience can easily relate) to the wider implications of the subject. If you are trying to argue a case your talk might be planned to deal with the opposing viewpoint followed by your own views. You will want to keep your audience interested all the way through your talk so you may decide to deal with some minor points first, building up to the main and most interesting point at the end. Any of these approaches, as well as several others, can work successfully – the important thing is that the main body of your talk should have an internal logic with one idea flowing naturally on to the next.

Once you have noted down headings for the main divisions and sub-divisions of your talk, look at them critically. Will the areas you intend to cover tell your audience the kind of information they will want to know and understand and find interesting? Will the talk as a whole appear logical and well balanced? Will it fulfil your aims? Play around with the framework of your talk until you are happy with it.

Obtaining and checking facts

Having planned out the framework of your talk, you will probably have become aware of gaps in your knowledge, and there will almost certainly be facts and perhaps quotations that you wish to use, which need checking. It is important that you check and double-check your facts, so that you can feel quite confident during your talk – you don't want doubts crossing your mind and interfering with your train of thought. Also, if the audience spots a fact that is obviously wrong, they are likely to be sceptical about the rest. Don't forget that facts such as populations and boundaries change, so your references must be authoritative and up-to-date. If you are talking on a subject connected with your job you will probably have most of the sources you need to check your facts and fill in gaps fairly easily to hand. If not, you may need to use your local reference library or a more specialist library. For some facts you may need to approach an acknowledged expert. You obviously cannot expect the expert or the librarian to do your research for you, but they should be willing to help with a genuine enquiry, and their specialist knowledge of sources could save you hours of searching. Don't forget that magazines and newspapers can often provide topical and up-to-date information.

It is usually best to tackle the research systematically, dealing with one aspect at a time. Always keep in mind the level and type of information you require. You can, of course, digress in your research if you've got plenty of time. However, it could mean that parts of your talk are poorly researched, or that you do not leave yourself time to plan your speech in detail or practise it. If you make notes, do make sure you make them accurately; for the sake of accuracy, it could be more satisfactory to take photocopies or cuttings (and to highlight the important and relevant facts, so that you can find them easily). Make sure that you note the sources of all your facts in case you want to refer back later, and develop a suitable system for filing all the information so that it is easily retrievable.

If you are arguing a particular point in your talk you need to be familiar with the opposition's views so that you can explain why these views should not be accepted. It is therefore just as important – and possibly more so – to collect information on the opposition's views than material with which you agree.

Obviously, your research may unearth a major topic you feel you must include in your talk. If this is the case you will have to amend your overall plan accordingly. However, on the whole, it is best to stick to the main framework you have already worked out rather than risk upsetting the balance and ending up with an unsuitable talk which includes facts that are not relevant.

More detailed planning
Having armed yourself with an overall framework for your talk and a good supply of accurate facts, you are now in a position to compose your talk in detail. Ideally, you should start this detailed planning a couple of weeks or so before the talk so that you do not need to rush too much at the last minute. If you are inexperienced at public speaking you will

probably find it easiest to write out your talk in full. This is not so that you can read it at the event or even learn it by heart, but so that you can feel confident that you have a good talk to give. Also, the actual mechanics of putting your ideas on paper will help clarify many thoughts and phrases as well as helping you to remember them. Having written out the talk in full, you will then need to produce a set of note cards to use at the talk itself. Some people may find they prefer to skip the writing out stage, and practice straight from note cards. Whichever method you use, there are certain points you should keep in mind.

First, and perhaps the most obvious, while composing your talk you need to consider your aims and audience. Think about what they will want, or need, to know, and aim to answer their unspoken questions. Consider what kind of information your audience is most likely to find interesting. Also keep in mind the quantity of information they are likely to be able to absorb; obviously a serious 'lecture' will have a lot more facts than a more light-hearted 'talk', but even in a lecture you may have to select carefully so that you do not end up with an extremely dry list of facts, most of which will go in one ear and out of the other! You want to aim to talk 'with' your audience not 'at' them, so where possible use examples that link everyone's common experiences. Audiences tend to dislike speakers acting as if they are superior when they obviously are not, but then again, some speakers try too hard to be 'one of the crowd' and this is not always popular either.

Audiences expect to be able to understand talks rather than marvel at the speaker's eloquence, so you should try to use simple straightforward words and phrases. This can be taken to extremes, but short, everyday words and sentences of simple construction will be easier for your audience to listen to as well as easier for you to remember. Why say 'I am at present unable to furnish an answer as to why...' when 'I don't know why...' will do just as well? Another common example of long-windedness is 'At this moment in time'. What's wrong with 'Now'? As well as using short words wherever possible, you should also make sure your words are of the right proportion. Adjectives are important to give colour to a talk, but an over-intense adjective before almost every noun rather cheapens the effect as well as making the talk much longer and more complicated than it really needs to be.

Humour is used more in social-type speeches than in talks and lectures, but even the most serious talk can often be lightened by a little well-thought-out and appropriate humour. Humour is best used to emphasise points rather than to impart information, and in particular can be useful in reminding audiences how not to do certain things. However, there are three important points to keep in mind when thinking about using humour. Firstly, is it relevant? Secondly, does it suit your style of speaking? Thirdly, does it suit that particular audience? 'Humour' should never be dragged in if it isn't relevant – after all you've been invited as a speaker not a comedian. The type of humour should relate to the type of person you are; if you are not the type who can tell jokes or anecdotes successfully in private life, you are unlikely to succeed in doing so in a talk! However, you may be the kind of person who appreciates the witty and apt phrase – if so concentrate on this kind of humour in your talks. Matching your humour to your audience is often more difficult, as you may have little idea of who will be there, and certainly no idea of what kind of mood they are in, until the talk itself. The best maxim to follow is 'if in doubt, leave it out'.

Apt and witty phrases are short and easily remembered, and are popular with most audiences. Jokes and anecdotes tend to be rather more difficult to use successfully. Anecdotes should be your own originals (even if your family has heard them umpteen times), as otherwise you run the risk that some of the audience have already heard the same story, perhaps with slight variations, and perhaps better told! Audiences will almost certainly see through someone else's anecdote passed off as your own and will not thank you for it. In 'talks', as opposed to social speeches, it is probably wiset to avoid jokes altogether.

Slang and swearing, like humour, must be treated with great care. You may be tempted to use them to make you appear 'with it' or more relaxed than you really are, but they may well offend or upset some of your audience. They may form an integral part of an anecdote, but the best course is probably to play safe and leave them out.

There are other features of talks which also need some

care and consideration. Quotations must, of course, be used accurately, but they should also be used sparingly. Someone may have summed up your views in a particularly fine way, but do remember that it is *your* knowledge and views that the audience wants to hear; they could just as easily look through a book of quotations at home. Metaphors, similies and analogies can also be very useful to put over certain points but, like quotations, should be used in moderation. Instead of just giving a height in feet or metres, why not go on to compare it with the height of a well-known building? Distances can be given in terms of the distance between two towns familiar to the audience, and populations compared with the population of the place where you are giving the talk.

If you plan to use visual aids such as slides to accompany your talk you will also need to bear this in mind while writing. Showing slides takes time so you will not be able to say as much in the same time as in a non-illustrated talk. Also the choice of slides or other visual aids tends to dictate what you say although, as stressed in the section on visual aids, you should aim to have a talk which could still go ahead even if some disaster befell the visual side at the last minute.

Committing yourself to paper

Having read through the last few pages of warnings you are probably reluctant to commit anything to paper. Don't worry. Just remember what you can and get started. Although it may seem logical to start with the introduction (and this is the order in which the notes below are given), it's often the most difficult part, so you may do better to make a start on the main body of the talk and come back to the Introduction later. Include the headings for the main sections of the talk even though you won't actually use these in the talk itself. Whether you type or write out your talk, do leave yourself plenty of space between lines. Use double or even triple spacing on a typewriter and only use one side of the paper. This will enable you to make amendments to the draft without too many confusing arrows, or even cut out sentences or paragraphs and physically put them somewhere else in the draft. If you have access to a word processor, you could of course work on your draft talks on the machine just as you would with any other piece of writing. But, do remember you are writing down something to be spoken, and use abbreviated forms such as 'I'd' rather than 'I would'.

In order to write out your talk you'll need to know roughly how many words will be needed. If you take an average talking speed as being about 120–130 words a minute you can multiply this by the length of the talk. You will probably be surprised how short a 30 or 40 minute talk looks when written out. An illustrated talk will be even shorter. You will also need to decide just how much time to allow for each part. Most speakers (and audiences) tend to agree that in a short talk you can allow up to a third of the time available for the introduction and conclusion combined, but on longer talks (over half an hour or so) a maximum of about 5 minutes each is enough. The divisions of the main body of your talk don't have to be all the same length; it's more important that they say just what is necessary clearly and concisely.

The introduction

The very first words of your talk will probably be 'Mr Chairman, Ladies and Gentlemen'. This is usually straightforward enough, but if you know you will have titled people present, or there will be special guests who should be acknowledged by name, do consult the section on forms of address (Chapter 2) and, if necessary, seek advice.

Following that, there are several different ways of getting into your talk. Probably the easiest approach for the beginner is a straightforward explanation of your plans for the talk. Although the title of the talk and a very brief biography should have been given in the chairman's introduction, half the audience probably weren't listening properly, so some repetition here won't do any harm. If necessary, you can acknowledge the repetition by saying something like 'As Mr X said in his introduction, the subject of my talk tonight is . . .'. You could then go on to give details of how you became interested in this subject or could outline how you propose to tackle the subject in your talk.

If you are talking on a little known or controversial subject you may need to use the introduction to give the audience the facts required to appreciate and understand the main body of the talk.

Besides being the time to provide background information for the rest of the talk, the introduction is also the time when you will be aiming to instil in the audience a feeling of confidence in you. Don't therefore use apologetic or falsely modest phrases; you'll only sow seeds of doubt in the audience's minds and they'll end up watching the way you talk, half expecting disasters, rather than concentrating on what you are actually saying.

Other ways of starting your talk include points of topical, local or historical interest. Topical points, perhaps something you have read on the subject in a recent newspaper, will help to make your talk seem fresh and up-to-date, while introducing something of local interest will show the audience that you have taken the trouble to angle your talk specifically towards them. If your talk is connected with an anniversary or similar event, an historical approach might be appropriate – perhaps something to do with attitudes towards the subject X years ago. The use of some kind of visual aid, perhaps a spectacular slide or specimen, is also a good way to excite the audience's interest.

Some of the other types of introduction which are often suggested are probably best left to the more experienced speaker. Humour or the use of a startling phrase or question can sometimes work well as they give the audience notice that this is going to be a lively and amusing talk.

So, in a summary, the best advice for beginners is to keep your introduction short, simple and straightforward.

The main body of the talk

Little extra needs to be said on this except that you should arrange your material so as to hold the interest of the audience throughout. Don't therefore use all your good material at the beginning of the talk, and do try to have interesting beginnings and ends to the parts of the talk within the main body. Also, try to guide your audience through the talk, and let them know when you are changing to another aspect of the subject by providing suitable linking phrases. Something like 'Alternatively' or 'There is another aspect', will probably sound better than 'Which reminds me of' or 'Which brings me to'; these tend to sound false unless you actually look as if you have just been reminded of the subject.

Also remember that your audience will be listening to, rather than reading, your talk. This means that they will not be able to go back to remind themselves what went before. You will therefore need to repeat yourself more often than in written material if they are to understand and remember the main points. As long as you do not pepper your talk with too many 'As I said's', they will probably not even notice the repetition, and will just think you gave a good clear talk.

The conclusion

Try to make your conclusion positive and constructive. Reiterate your main point or points, especially if you are not giving a summing up after any questions. If the aim of your talk is to get the audience to do something, this is the time to mention it so that it is the thought with which they go home.

As with the introduction, the conclusion is a time when many inexperienced speakers are prone to get too apologetic. Assume that the audience has enjoyed your talk and not found it boring, and don't sow doubts in their minds by phrases such as 'If I may take up a little more of your time' or 'You've sat still and listened to me for quite long enough so I'll now just sum up my conclusions'. If you feel some introductory phrase is necessary, something simple like 'Finally, or 'In conclusion' is usually quite adequate.

Amending your draft

If you have not done so already, the first thing to do is to read your draft aloud at a suitable pace, and then time it. You will then know whether you need to cut or add to your draft as you make your amendments. If it is too short don't be tempted to pad it out with 'waffle'; find some extra relevant information which actually adds something to the talk. If your draft is too long you may be able to shorten it sufficiently by cutting out unnecessary adjectives or phrases, but if it is much too long you would do better to cut out some of the less interesting and relevant sentences or paragraphs. Talking for longer than required is one sin you must not commit; besides the discourtesy of upsetting the programme, you may find half your audience has fallen asleep by the time you reach the most important points towards the end!

This is the stage at which you must be very critical with your draft. Read it through as many times as possible and consider whether everything in it is relevant and interesting. Look out for jargon or abbreviations which may need explanation, and words or phrases incorrectly used. A talk does not have to have perfect grammar, and some people would argue that a speaker should reflect a common (but often ungrammatical) usage. However, any obviously bad grammar may irritate some of the audience and discourage them from listening to what you have to say. Also check that your arguments are logically presented and that the talk contains no material likely to offend.

It is often worth putting the draft on one side for a few days between revisions; coming back to it afresh, you will almost certainly notice something new. Once you feel you have produced a 'final' version, time yourself again to check that the talk is about the right length. Then, unless you have very few changes, type or write it out again so that you have a clean copy from which to practise your talk.

Visual aids

Discussion of the use of visual aids has been left until after the section on writing out your talk, because in most cases a talk should be able to stand on its own without props. You are likely to be more confident if you know you could still give your audience a talk, albeit a shorter one, even if something went wrong on the visual side. The term visual *aids*, itself, emphasises that they are only a support, and brilliant illustrations won't save an otherwise bad talk. However, something visual does help to put across certain points which are not easily explained in words. Imagine, for example, trying to discuss a painting without visual help. Visual aids can also be useful to enliven and add emphasis to a talk. Slides are usually the first type of visual aid that comes to mind, and a few points about their use are given below. However, you may also want to consider using films or videos, maps, models and plans, diagrams or actual specimens. Don't mix too many types of visual aid within one talk as it will probably be rather distracting, and do check that suitable equipment is available. (This includes adequate black-out facilities if it is a day-time talk.) Also make sure that anything visual you intend to use will be able to be seen by the whole audience. Otherwise, you will alienate the unfortunate people at the back of the room. If you are talking about something small such as postcards or fossils, for example, get slides showing some of the most important or interesting types to use during the talk. You could always put out a display of actual specimens for people to look at afterwards. It is best to avoid passing specimens round during a talk as this tends to be distracting, and again the poor unfortunates at the back get the specimen only when you are several points further on and they've forgotten what particular feature they are supposed to be looking for!

Readability and clarity must also be kept in mind if you are considering using slides with written material on them. Restrict yourself to very few words in large lettering, and do test the slide out before the talk if at all possible. A couple of other points must be borne in mind when considering whether to use a slide. Firstly, does it actually put over the point you are trying to make? Secondly, is it visually and technically satisfactory and able to stand up to projection? There is a tendency among speakers to use a slide just because they feel they ought to have an illustration, but an audience is soon going to get irritated by a series of poor, irrelevant, out of focus, bleached or dark slides. Another irritating factor in some illustrated talks is the 'slide that got away'. This is where the speaker shows a series of slides, perhaps of something like the restoration of a building, but doesn't have the vital first or last shot.

If you are using visual material as part of your talk you will need to mark on your speech, and eventually your note cards, where you intend to bring this material in. If there is a long gap between slides plan to use a blank slide rather than leaving up the previous or next slide, since this will only be distracting. Alternatively, switch off the projector and ask for the lights to be put on. However, switching the projector and lights on and off is, itself, distracting so you should try to arrange your slides in one, or at most two, blocks. If possible you should practise giving the talk actually using the slides, and if you can persuade a friend or relative to help they could give you useful feedback on your technique. Some of the bad habits you may have could include a tendency to wander in front of the screen or wave the pointer around in a distracting manner. You also need to practise using any long-distance control mechanism smoothly (so that you do not irritatingly flick in and out of focus or go backwards instead of forwards). Incidentally, this kind of control is much less distracting for the audience than any kind of signal to a projectionist, so you should use a projector with this facility if at all possible.

Making note cards

If you have written out a draft of your talk in full, the easiest way of working towards your note cards is to go through a copy of the final version and underline or highlight the headings plus key phrases that you are keen not to forget. If you feel it would help, you may also wish to mark the first and last sentences of each section of the talk so that you can be reminded of these. However, you must be selective as otherwise your notes will be almost as long as the written out talk! Once you have marked the points that you hope to include on your note cards, try and compress each point to a single word or short phrase. If you have not gone through the stage of writing out a draft, your note cards will need to be based directly on the framework you worked out earlier.

Most speakers find postcards or index cards 6 x 4 inches (150 x 100mm) or 8 x 5 inches (200 x 130mm) the best material on which to make their notes. Paper tends to be too flimsy, and is liable to collapse as you are in the middle of reading from it, or else rustles annoyingly into the microphone. You should aim to use one card for each major section of your talk. For a longer talk this will probably work out at about one card per 10 or 15 minutes. It is important to complete any notes for a particular section on one card so that you can turn to your next card at a natural pause in your talk.

You will need to type or write very clearly on your cards so that they are easy to read. Write on only one side of the cards and also leave plenty of space between notes. Within these constraints you might like to develop a system with different coloured inks, highlighting, underlining and layout, to help you identify different types of notes. For example you could perhaps underline the main section headings in red, leaving subsections alone, and perhaps list notes to remind you of slides at an appropriate place in a separate column to the right. It may also be useful to use numbers and letters for your main headings and subheadings. Whatever system you use, keep it simple so that you don't forget what is what, and do check that you can read everything and pick out any colour coding used when you hold the card low down (at about stomach height) in poorish light.

You will probably find you have room on each card to list the main heading plus two or three subheadings, and perhaps two or three main points within each of these. Wherever possible use a single word or short phrase to remind you of an idea. The only exception to this is any quotation – if you are noting these on your cards you should copy the quotations carefully in full. However, it is often best to use either the original publication with the page and passage clearly marked, or to photocopy the passage and stick it to a separate card. If you clearly number the marker slips or the individual passages on the quotations card, you can then just use the wording, 'Quote 1', etc., on the main note cards.

Once you have produced a set of note cards number them in order. It may also be worth fixing them together in some way so that they are kept in order and do not get lost. Many speakers find 'Treasury Tags' through one or two holes a good method. If you wish you can make such a system more sophisticated – for example you could add tabs to the cards to help avoid the danger of turning over two cards at once. If you know you will be speaking from behind a table, you may wish to add a final blank card which can be folded in half to enable you to 'stand' your cards on the table. A blank final card can also be useful if you likely to want to note any ideas that occur to you during any preceeding talks, or even during your own. However, if an earlier talk suggests something you wish to add into your talk it is better to include a note to remind you at an appropriate point on the main cards.

Practising

You may wish to start practising your speech by reading it aloud from your full written-out version, but as soon as possible you should try to manage with just your note cards. By the time you have got to this stage you should be fairly familiar with what you have written and you will probably be pleasantly surprised by how much you remember. Try to rehearse in a convincing set-up. Stand up and do not attempt to compete with the television or other distractions. If you know you will be using a microphone, or will have a lectern or table and chair to contend with, try to rig up appropriate conditions so that at least you are familiar with the physical constraints with which you may be faced. If you are giving a slide talk, you should obviously practise with slides. Early on, you will probably feel less self-conscious if you practise alone, but once you have become more confident you might like to ask some friends or relatives to act as an audience. They will probably be more offputting than any other audience, though, so avoid doing this if you think they will merely diminish your confidence. However, do try to imagine an audience in front of you and practise speaking at a suitable voice level. If you find you are having trouble remembering all the points in your talk, you may find it helps to first practise giving a much shorter talk in which you just amplify the notes on your cards very slightly. This should help you to get the main points firmly fixed in your mind. You can then go on to practise giving a fuller talk. Try to cultivate the ability to see what you are describing in your 'mind's eye' – this is particularly important to enable you to tell anecdotes well.

Once you are reasonably confident that you can remember all you wish to say with the aid of your note cards, you can then concentrate more on your actual presentation. At this stage it is a good idea to tape record, or even video, yourself, or to ask a trusted friend to listen and watch critically. You will almost certainly find you have some bad habits in your presentation – almost all speakers do – but at least if you know about them you can do your best to cure them.

Improving your presentation

Oral presentation
In the section earlier in this chapter dealing with planning and writing out your talk there were warnings about using clichés or long-winded words and phrases. You probably eliminated them at that stage but, reached the stage of talking directly from your note cards, you may well note a tendency for such phrases to creep back in. You'll probably be aware of some of these yourself, but a friend can be particularly useful in picking up phrases you had not noticed.

Guard against vagueness and gabbling words and phrases like 'you know what I mean', 'and so on' or 'etcetera'. This happens when the brain races ahead of the voice. Try to slow down and be more specific.

Timing and pauses are vital to the successful presentation of a talk. Don't be afraid of properly used pauses, and never fill them in with 'ers' and 'ums' or 'you know's'. Instead try to make use of pauses – they can help make a point more dramatic, or can simply help to structure the talk so that the audience is aware that you are now changing direction. A varying voice tone helps to structure a talk and makes it easier to listen to – if you find you are talking rather monotonously you may find it helps to try and visualise what you are talking about a little more. This lets your natural emotions introduce more variety into your voice.

Other points to watch out for and improve include poor pronunciation, a tendency to tail away at the end of sentences, and use of phrases that could be misinterpreted. 'Being a wet day, I stayed inside', might sound perfectly logical to you and most of your audience, but offputting sniggers could be produced by misinterpretation.

Visual presentation
Unless you have the opportunity to practise your talk in front of a video camera, the best way to find out if you have any irritating mannerisms is to ask a friend to be honest with you. If you are nervous you may tend to move around rather a lot, shifting from one foot to another, swaying, or even pacing back and forth. Alternatively you may have been

warned about fidgety speakers and may stand far too rigidly, as if at attention. Most people find it easiest to stand with their feet slightly apart, and with their weight over the balls of their feet. In general, the less formal the talk, the more movement is acceptable, but if you do move around make sure your movements are related to changes in the talk and don't just wander around aimlessly. If you are using a fixed microphone you should confine movements to pauses, otherwise your voice level is likely to fluctuate up and down.

Hands always tend to be a problem. The classic mistake to avoid is putting your hands in your pockets and fiddling with keys or coins, which jangle irritatingly. However, in addition to finding their way into pockets, hands are prone to other bad habits. Pushing hair away from your face or taking spectacles on and off can be particularly distracting if repeated throughout a talk. You should also avoid holding your hands and arms too rigidly at your side or folded in front of you. If you have a lectern at a suitable height, you would probably do best to rest your hands gently on either side – but don't grip the lectern tensely as if it were a lifeboat saving you from drowning! Alternatively keep your hands occupied in holding your notes – loosely in front of you for most of the time then use one hand to lift the notes to reading level as necessary.

Gesticulation can add life to a talk, but it can also easily become irritating. Gesticulate only where it is appropriate to the talk and helps to put over emotion. The larger the audience the more generous the gesticulation can be, but beware of thumping tables – your practice table may take the treatment but the table on the night may collapse under the pressure!

Slide talks have their own particular hazards. Besides obvious problems like a tendency to walk in front of the screen or to talk to the screen rather than the audience, mannerisms such as turning round all the time to check that the slide is still there can soon become annoying.

Practice makes perfect!

Once you have identified any bad habits, practise again and try to improve your presentation. If you are an inexperienced speaker it is probably impossible to practise too much as your 'nerves' on the night will probably compensate for any overfamiliarity with the talk. So practise until you are as confident as possible or until the date itself puts an end to your preparations. But do remember you are not trying to learn your talk, merely to reassure yourself that you can give it from your note cards. If you are more experienced, you may feel that too much practice will make your talk sound stale, if so, two or three run-throughs, one preferably in front of an audience, will probably suffice. Don't forget also that although you may have heard your speech several times, it will still be the first time for your audience.

Final checks with the organiser

About a week or so before the talk, you should contact the organiser to confirm the details you were given earlier and to make any final arrangements. In particular, confirm the length of time for which you are required to speak and also check the chairman's name – this may not be the same. Also ask for the telephone number of the venue, if it has one, just in case you have any last-minute delays. If you need special equipment, make sure it will be available, and also warn the organiser if you will need help to carry your own equipment from your car. With warning he may be able to arrange for an able-bodied and willing helper to be there early.

If you are driving to the venue, make sure you are certain of how to find the building and also check where you will be able to park. If possible, and especially if you have heavy equipment, ask the organiser to reserve a parking spot for you near the entrance. If you are travelling by public transport you will need to arrange to be met at the train or bus station unless the venue is within easy walking distance or you are sure of being able to get a taxi.

Deciding what to wear

If you are not certain what kind of dress is appropriate for the function ask the organiser well in advance. If in doubt it is better to be over rather than underdressed for the occasion, and you should also err towards the conventional rather than the outrageous. Avoid wearing a new outfit at your talk, and if possible give yourself a dress-rehearsal so that you can identify any potential problems. In particular make sure that your feet and throat feel comfortable – avoid anything too tight in either area. Also avoid wide, flowing sleeves if there is likely to be any danger of you sweeping a glass or your notes off the table with them. Large or pendulous jewellery is also hazardous and distracting – both because of the flickering of light on metallic items and because of the jangling noises bracelets can make. Once you have settled on what you intend to wear, make sure it is all clean and well pressed in plenty of time.

Getting ready

Although you are the most vital part of the talk, you will need to check that you have the various other items with you, especially if you are giving a talk with visual aids. This may sound rather like a parental nag before sending children off to school, but do check you have such items as money for any travelling expenses (as well as small change for telephone calls and parking), a handkerchief, a notebook and pencil, a comb and, of course, your note cards. Make sure your watch is correct, and if you will be driving to the talk don't forget to check the car in advance to minimise the chances of delays *en route*.

If you are using slides or other visual aids, you will need to check that any equipment you are taking is working well. It is also advisable to take two spare bulbs for the projector and an extension lead and adapter in case the power sources in the room are not all you were led to believe. If possible, load the slide magazine(s) beforehand. A useful mnenomic to remind you of checks for your slides is W.O.W. (right *Way* round, right *Order*, right *Way* up). If you get into the habit of marking all your slides with a small dot in their bottom left corners (as they are held for normal viewing), it will be easy to check they are all correct. If you plan to use a blackboard or to pin up diagrams, take your own chalk and drawing pins as such items have a habit of disappearing just when you need them.

Finally, allow yourself plenty of time for travelling to the venue.

4. Presenting a Talk

Pre-talk checks

Aim to arrive in plenty of time for your talk. If the worst happens and your car breaks down or your train is running late do try to contact the organiser so that he knows you may be late. If all goes according to plan, however, and you do arrive early, you may find it helpful to go for a short walk around the area. Besides giving you time to relax a little after travelling, you will be able to absorb a little of the feel of the place and the people. This is all useful background knowledge which will help you pitch your talk correctly and may also provide you with local examples which you can bring into your talk.

You should already know the name of the organiser or chairman, so when you go into the venue try to find them first. It is probably best to do any setting up of equipment as soon as you can. Once again, if possible, allow yourself more time than you think necessary in case of any hitches. Even if you have no equipment to set up, at least ask to look at the room in which you will be speaking, and also make sure you know where the toilet is. Also check where you will be sitting and that you have been provided with the basic equipment you expected in the way of table, blackboard and chalk (and wiper), a glass of water, etc. Look at the lighting, too; will you have sufficient light to see your notes, and have the organisers thought to check that none of the lights shine straight into your eyes or into those of the audience? If you can spot any potential problems before the audience come in it may be possible to do something about them.

Even if you are using a microphone, it is a good idea to test the acoustics of the room before the talk. If your voice sounds absorbed and muffled, the acoustics are probably rather 'soft'. The bodies and clothes of the audience, when they arrive, also tend to absorb sound so you should look

47

and see if there is any way in which the room can be given more reflective surfaces. Perhaps curtains could be drawn back if they are not necessary for blacking out the room. If, on the other hand, the room has 'hard' acoustics with lots of echoes from the reflective surfaces, the opposite technique is needed. If echoing is very bad, try to use your voice as deliberately as possible and make good use of pauses so that the echoes do not get confused with your next statement.

If you are using a microphone you should definitely test it out before your talk. This is best done with a helper. Ask your helper to stand normally and to talk into the microphone in his normal voice while you move around the hall. By this means you should be able to judge the best volume, speed of talking, and position of the microphone and loudspeakers (if they are moveable). You may need to have some microphones within 3 to 4 inches of your face while others may respond better if you are about 18 – 24 inches away – each microphone seems to have its own idiosyncrasies. Watch out for 'dead spots' between two or more speakers. Then try using the microphone yourself, and ask your helper to make similar checks. Test by using typical sentences, not, 'One-two-three-testing'. If your helper does not know what is about to be said it is easier for him to judge whether or not you can be heard clearly. If you are the only speaker at the event, make sure the microphone is at the correct height – just below chin level is about right – and also that it is pointing slightly upwards. If you are one of several speakers, make sure you know how the adjustments work so that you can alter the microphone to suit yourself as unobtrusively as possible.

If you are using any visual aids, you will also need to set them up beforehand. Try to find some way of keeping any specimens or diagrams completely out of sight until they are needed, otherwise you may find the audience are looking at them rather than listening to you. But don't just hide specimens under a cloth on the table. The mysterious shapes will intrigue and distract the audience even more than the objects themselves. If you are using a projector and screen get everything set up and tested, and if it is an unusual projector practise using any long-distance control mechanism. Alternatively, make sure that you have agreed a cue with the projectionist for slide changes. You can simply say 'next slide please' as necessary, and other methods include the use of a 'clicker' held in the speaker's hand, or a doorbell-type buzzer attached to the table or lectern. Some speakers provide the projectionist with a marked-up copy of the script of their talk. However, the latter method can fall to pieces if you deviate much from your planned talk or if the projectionist does not listen carefully.

Having dealt with the equipment you have done almost all you can by way of thorough preparation. You can then spend the rest of the time until the talk chatting to people. Once again, confirm the programme details to make sure there have been no last-minute changes. Also, make sure that the person who will be introducing you (usually the chairman) has all the details he needs. It is often helpful to provide the chairman with a note listing your name (as you wish it to be used), where you are from and/or who you represent, your qualifications for giving this talk (just relevant experience, not a whole potted biography), and the title of the talk. A competent chairman will probably want to check these details with you anyway, and an accurate and informative introduction will help get the meeting off to a good start. If you feel it would help, ask the chairman to warn you about five minutes before the end of your allotted time. That way you can arrange a discreet signal between yourselves which will be less obvious than people pointedly looking at their watches as you start to overrun!

You may well be offered an alcoholic drink before the start of a talk. Such a drink may have the immediate effect of making you feel less nervous, but do treat pre-talk drinks with extreme caution. Besides the dangers of the alcohol suddenly hitting you in the middle of your talk causing such effects as slow, muddled thoughts, slurred speech or the introduction of impromptu humour in bad taste, you could also find yourself becoming reliant on a pre-talk drink, and may be put off if one is not available. Be especially wary if you are taking any drugs for medical reasons, as these could add to the hazards of drink.

Getting started

If, as the moment of truth arrives, you find your nerves getting the better of you try to breathe slowly, deeply and steadily. This should help you to relax, both because it increases the supply of oxygen to your muscles and other organs, and because while you are concentrating your attention on your breathing you are unable to worry about other things at the same time!

For most talks, you will probably enter the room or walk up on to the platform with the chairman and other officials after the audience has assembled. Try to walk confidently (neither too briskly, nor too casually) and glance and smile at the audience. Take the seat indicated to you, and if a table is provided arrange your notes and any other material in front of you. Even if you are extremely nervous try not to let it show in a frenzied gripping of the arm rests or by legs twisted round the chair legs or one another. Also remember that the microphone may already be switched on and if so will pick up any asides or nervous jangling of coins or clicking of ball-point pens.

You should do the chairman the courtesy of listening to his short, introductory speech just as you hope he will listen to yours. Don't sit there shuffling through your notes or staring intently at the floor wishing it would swallow you up. Instead, look at the chairman and the audience and try to gauge their moods. If you haven't been able to test the acoustics beforehand, you may be able to judge the volume you will need to use by observing whether all the audience can hear the introduction. If your throat has suddenly gone dry, take a sip or two of water. If you are ever in the position of not being introduced do your own introduction. It is not immodest to explain why you are qualified to give the talk, and gives the audience useful background information.

When the introduction comes to an end with a phrase such as '. . . so, Ladies and Gentlemen, I would like you to welcome Mr Frederick Jones', do not jump up immediately. Try to judge when the applause is beginning to die away and then stand up and push your chair out of your way so that it is not digging into the backs of your legs. Slow and deliberate movements will make you look, as well as feel, calmer. Wait until the audience is quiet, and then start with the formal opening address. In most cases you should have been able to decide in advance the appropriate words to use. As you address the chairman, and then the audience, do look at them. Then you are into the talk itself. For the first few minutes your audience will be assessing you and perhaps thinking that you look younger or fatter than they expected, or they may be admiring your choice of dress. You should also be assessing them. Do they look eager or bored, and do they look as if they can all hear you clearly?

The rest of the talk

You will probably feel a lot happier once you have got started and have discovered that the audience is not going to shout you down, fall asleep or burst into giggles. All you then have to do is deliver the rest of the talk. Don't worry too much about all the do's and don'ts given earlier – if you have practised thoroughly, you will hopefully do most things right without even thinking about them. No talk is ever perfect, and you will almost certainly notice more 'bad bits' than the audience does. If you find you are still tending to shake a little, however, don't make the problem worse by leaning on a flimsy table or anything else which may shake in sympathy!

One aspect that is difficult to practise beforehand is ways of responding to the audience and making them all feel involved. Do watch your audience carefully and try to respond to the way they are reacting. Don't just stare straight ahead, but from time to time glance to the sides as well as the front and back so that all the audience feel they have been addressed personally. If you are using a fixed microphone, however, do this with care and preferably during pauses or otherwise you will probably find your voice level fluctuating.

If you make an error or blunder during your talk there are two ways of dealing with it. If you realise immediately that you have said something wrong, deal with the error straight-away. If, for example, you realise you have misquoted the population of some town you could say something like 'Sorry, the population of X should, of course, have been Y thousand rather than Y million'. If, however, you realise that you made an error much earlier in the talk it is best to ignore it rather than confusing the audience by referring back to an earlier point. You could correct an error made during the main body of the talk as you pause before the conclusion, or you could straighten the record at question time. But don't interrupt the flow of your talk at any other time. If you temporarily lose track of where you are, a similar strategy should be followed. Either deal with it immediately and stop, apologise and look at your cards, or otherwise ignore your hesitation and hope the audience did not notice.

Outside noises, such as a pneumatic drill in the road nearby or the clattering of cups in an adjacent room, are unpredictable hazards with which you may have to deal. If the noise is a constant rumble you may be able to deal with it just by raising your voice level slightly. Intermittent and loud noises are more of a problem. Don't try to ignore them. If you think you can overcome them, make some comment that acknowledges the disturbance and then carry on. If the interruption is too bad, you would do best to stop and see if the noise can be quietened down. You may then need to backtrack a little to cover points which may not have been heard clearly during the interruption.

If you are the kind of person who is good at impromptu humour, you may wish to add comments as they occur to you on the day. Impromptu humour can help to make a talk fresh and spontaneous but, as with all humour, handle it with care and, keeping your audience in mind, exercise your own censoring mechanism. Don't let spontaneous humour in a talk be at the expense of the audience or the venue – most of the audience may laugh with you, but you will almost certainly put someone's back up.

Aggressive heckling is unlikely in a straightforward, non-controversial talk, and any interruptions from the audience are more likely to be questions. If you can deal with the point very briefly without interrupting the flow of the talk, do so. If, however, the question needs a more detailed answer you would probably do best to suggest that the questioner asks you about that point again during question time. In some informal talks the speaker may actually invite questions during the talk, but in this case the programming should have allowed for this so that fuller answers can be given without disturbing the schedule.

Finally, on the subject of time, you should always aim to

stop before the audience wants you to stop. Your practice talks should have given you an idea of roughly how long each part of the talk should take. If you find you are running over time see if there is a bit that could be missed out or something which could be explained more briefly without losing the basic structure of the talk. This is better than rushing through or drastically cutting the final part when you find you have ten minutes' worth of talk to squeeze into five minutes or less. If your talk takes less time than you had planned, don't worry or try to pad it out with waffle. The audience are unlikely to mind a shorter talk, and the extra time can always be used for more questions.

Question time

Most talks end with a round of applause then question time, when members of the audience can ask the speaker for clarification of points they did not understand or can ask for more information on subjects they found particularly interesting. In formal meetings, the question time will be controlled by the chairman who will start by saying something to the effect that, 'Mr X has kindly agreed to answer any questions you may have.' If this is followed by a stony silence he will hopefully put a question of his own to get the session going. You yourself can always encourage questions by commenting when you make a controversial point in your talk: I've no doubt someone may want to come back at me on that at question time.' A good chairman will also deal with mumbled or unclear questions, repeating them so that both you and all the audience know what was asked. If he doesn't you should. Be particularly mindful of questions asked by somebody at the front of the room which cannot be heard at the back. He should also deal with unfairly aggressive or irrelevant questions. Having said that, not all chairmen are good chairmen, so you may be left to cope on your own.

At a formal meeting you should stand up and 'reply through the chair', that is, starting your reply 'Mr Chairman, Mr X asks if . . .' or similar. Address your reply to the whole audience, but look at the questioner fairly frequently.

If the questions are straightforward don't look too relieved, and try to appear courteous and interested even if the question seems trivial and unimportant. It may be the first time the questioner has dared to get to his feet and ask a question, and it is obviously important to him. Also deal with all questioners equally – just because someone is a civic dignitary or similar it doesn't mean that his question should get preferential treatment.

If you get difficult questions, don't waffle or pretend you know more than you do. You could be found out! Instead, admit you don't know, but be as helpful as you can. If, for example, you know you have the required information in a book at home, you could offer to take the questioner's name and address and contact him or her later with the information they require. But if you do make such an offer, don't forget to keep your promise.

When someone presents you with a long and complex question which is really two or three questions in one, it may help to note them down. You can then deal with them in the order asked, rather than dealing with one part of the question and then finding you have completely forgotten what the other parts of the question were.

You will almost certainly find that you are sometimes asked questions where the questioner is more interested in looking important or knowledgeable than in seeking information. Deal with such questions as courteously and briefly as you can. If someone provides some information you did not know, don't resent it but thank them. Similarly, if someone makes a valid criticism, accept it and ask for any suggestions the questioner may have. If they are genuine about it they may in fact give you useful suggestions. If they are just attempting to be self-important, such courteous treatment will probably stop them in their tracks.

Aggressive or persistent questioning is more likely in political or controversial public meetings than in talks to local societies. If the chairman doesn't deal with such questioners you could always try such techniques as 'I'm sorry I didn't quite catch all of that question', forcing the questioner to repeat the question. It is more difficult to be aggressive a second time.) Alternatively you could offer to talk to a persistent questioner after the main meeting in order to give the other members of the audience more time to put *their* questions.

After the talk

Your presence at the meeting may end with the vote of thanks and applause, but you may also be invited to socialise with members of the group afterwards. If so, do bear in mind that you are still 'on show' and creating an impression.

If you have to stay overnight after a talk, likewise be considerate and don't land the group a huge drinks bill from the hotel. Staying with members of the committee is often not very satisfactory from either side, but it may be the only option if the group has rather limited funds. However late you were kept up to answer more questions, or however early their boisterous children woke you up, do send your hosts a note of thanks afterwards.

Finally, when you do get home, you may find it useful to add details of the title, date and event (together with any impressions of how the talk went and how you could improve it) to your note cards. These will then form a useful record for future talks.

5. Types of Public Speaking

Short, 'formalised' speeches

This first section deals with short speeches which generally follow a set formula. You may get very little warning when you are asked to do such speaking, but for all except the Loyal Toast it may be worth jotting down a few notes just to remind you of what you intend to say. The remarks made in the section on preparing longer talks concerning speaking clearly and distinctly and avoiding too many 'ers' and 'ums', still apply, and you should also try to make sure that any nervousness does not lead you into too many clichéd phrases. Having said that, introducing and thanking speakers is fairly straightforward and is good practice for preparing and giving longer talks and speeches.

Introducing speakers

The speaker is usually introduced by the chairman of the group. An introduction should be very brief, at most two or three minutes as, after all, it is the speaker that everybody is there to hear. An introduction should comprise three parts: who the speaker is and who he represents; something about his background and qualifications for talking on the subject; and the title of the talk or speech. It is conventional to finish the introduction with a phrase along the lines, 'Ladies and Gentlemen, will you please welcome Mr X.' At that point the person making the introduction gestures to the speaker to rise and, having led the applause, sits down himself.

If you are making an introduction, you should check with the speaker before the meeting starts the pronunciation of his name and the version he would like you to use. This could be anything from just 'Fred' if he is someone already known to all the group, or 'Mr Frederick Jones' which is probably the most commonly used version, or 'Mr F Jones' or 'Dr Jones' if that is what the speaker prefers. With women speakers there are even more variations possible! Also ask the speaker for a few relevant biographical details, for example when and how he first became interested in the subject on which he is talking, and note them down so that you get the details right. It is also worth checking whether there is anything he *does not* want mentioned. If you have to introduce a well-known speaker you may be able to get some background information on them from publications such as *Who's Who*.

When the talk is due to start you will first have to gain everyone's attention by clapping your hands or banging on the table. Say something such as, 'Ladies and Gentlemen, could we now start our meeting', and then allow the audience a brief interval to get themselves settled and quiet before you launch into your introduction.

In your introduction it is best to try to avoid clichéd phrases such as 'The speaker needs no introduction'. If this is the case why are you giving one? Also don't try to predict what the speaker will cover. You may lead the audience to expect something completely different from what the speaker has in mind! Finally, although you obviously want to point out how much of an expert the speaker is, don't embarrass him by too great a build-up which he then feels unable to match.

Thanking speakers

The vote of thanks is usually proposed by a pre-arranged member of the audience from the floor and, like the introduction, it should be brief, lasting two to three minutes at the most. It should be introduced by the chairman, who will '. . . ask Mr X to give the vote of thanks'. A vote of thanks should sound spontaneous and genuine, and there is very little you can do to prepare for one as obviously you won't know what the talk is like until it has been given. Most votes of thanks start by saying that you are speaking on behalf of all the audience and then go on to say something complimentary about the quality or content of the talk. You can then perhaps mention one or two points you found particularly interesting. Finally, you propose the vote of thanks by saying something like, 'Ladies and Gentlemen, on behalf of us all I would like to thank Mr X.' Another, perhaps slightly clichéd but acceptable close is '. . . show our appreciation in the usual way.' You can then lead the applause and sit down.

Again, as with introductions, it is important that you get the speaker's name correct. Also try to choose original adjectives to describe the talk – the phrase 'an interesting talk' is sometimes regarded as damning with faint praise. If you can think of nothing complimentary to say about the talk itself, you could perhaps thank the speaker for the time and effort he has put into preparing and giving the talk to your group. You should *not* use the vote of thanks to take the speaker to task on something he has said nor to put forward your own views on the subject.

Occasionally a formal vote of thanks which is proposed and seconded may be taken, but this is very rare nowadays.

Other votes of thanks

The same principles as outlined above would apply to other situations such as giving a vote of thanks after an amateur dramatic society performance. In such a case you would do best to avoid singling out individual performers, but should thank the whole cast and also mention all the people helping backstage.

The Loyal Toast

The Loyal Toast is the first toast proposed after a formal dinner and is usually the responsibility of the chairman or president of the society holding the dinner. There is a convention that smoking is not permitted until after the Loyal Toast, so it should be proposed as soon as is reasonable after the final course of the meal. No speech should be given with the Loyal Toast. The toastmaster, if there is one, or otherwise the person announcing the Toast, should first bang on the table to call for order. You should then say something to the effect, 'Ladies and Gentlemen, I will now ask you to rise and join me in the Loyal Toast'. When everyone is standing, you should then lift your glass and say 'The Queen'. Everyone else then lifts their glasses, repeats 'The Queen', and then takes a sip of their drink. You should then announce, 'Ladies and Gentlemen you may now smoke', and sit down.

You can just stand and say 'The Queen', but it is generally better to ask people to stand and give them time to do so, otherwise you end up with only half the people on their feet by the time they are supposed to be drinking the toast. If you are the host or chairman, the only other point to bear in mind is the need to make sure that the glasses are filled shortly before the toast so that everyone has something with which to drink the Toast. At very formal dinners there may be a second Loyal Toast to the other members of the Royal Family (done in the same way), but this is not very common.

Grace
To avoid upsetting any particular religious groups a layman may sometimes be asked to say 'grace' before a dinner. 'For the food we are about to receive may we be truly thankful, Amen', would probably be acceptable in most cases. Whatever form of grace you say keep it short and avoid humour as well as Latin words which may not be understood by everyone present.

Social speaking
This section includes longer toasts and replies to them, after-dinner speeches, presentations and official openings. This type of speaking aims primarily to entertain, and you will usually have some time to prepare what you wish to say. Most of the points mentioned in the chapter on preparing for a longer talk will apply, but a little more humour and less fact would probably be appropriate. As most social speaking will last for only 10 to 15 minutes at the most, you should find it possible to make all the notes you require for your speech on one note card. Check what dress is appropriate, and if you will have to wear hired evening dress do try it on beforehand so that you feel reasonably comfortable and confident in it.

Toasts
After the Loyal Toast at a dinner or other function there may be a number of other toasts. These may include patriotic toasts, toasts to absent friends and toasts to the guests of honour. The usual complaint about toasts is that they go on too long. So, unless you have specifically been asked to talk for longer, you should try to restrict yourself to three to five minutes. It is difficult to advise what to include since there

are so many different types, but it is best only to deal with one topic connected with the group or person you are toasting. It may be appropriate to introduce some gentle humour, but relevant anecdotes are more suitable than jokes. Toasts at dinners generally start by addressing the chairman (or president), followed by any distinguished guests, then 'Ladies and Gentlemen'. Say everything else you have to say before asking for a toast, otherwise you may find some of the people present rising to drink the toast in the middle of your speech. Conversely, remember that the toast is the reason why you are speaking. Don't sit down after saying your piece and forget to propose it! Replies to toasts should be similarly brief and are dealt with, together with replies to presentations, later in this chapter.

Special features of some toasts are mentioned below.

Patriotic toasts
Patriotic toasts, to Her Majesty's Forces or one of the Forces in particular, are usually given only at events specifically connected with the armed forces. It is appropriate to be slightly patriotic, but this should not be overdone. If the proposer has served in one of the forces himself some gentle humour may be acceptable. The reply to a patriotic toast should be given by a serving member of one of the forces. He should not use the occasion to try and 'knock' the other forces, but should stress what they have in common.

The mayor and council
This toast may be given at civic dinners. As the mayor and council members may be known to many of those present, it is often possible to bring in a more personal element. For instance, if the Mayor is known to be passionately interested in cricket, some reference to this fact would be appropriate.

Our Member of Parliament
Toasts to MPs may be made at political party gatherings or at more general gatherings. If the latter is the case, the toast should be worded to avoid party politics so that it is acceptable to all present.

The Ladies

This toast is less common in these days of sex-equality, but when it does occur it is traditionally made by the youngest bachelor present. This toast should be light-hearted but flattering and in good taste.

Our Guests

If you are asked to toast the guests you should include some complimentary comment about the principal guest(s) including the person who is to reply to your toast.

The success of the society or club

This toast is commonly part of an annual club dinner and would be proposed by the chairman. He should thank the secretary (who usually replies to the toast) and the other officials for their support during the year. He could also mention some of the outstanding events of the previous year. As long as it has not figured too often in previous years he could perhaps base his toast on the club's motto.

Our opponents

The main theme behind a toast to sports opponents should be good sportsmanship. If your team won the game, it would be courteous to say something to the effect that the opponents did not give you an easy victory. If you lost, don't dwell on why that happened, but congratulate the winners and perhaps end by suggesting light-heartedly that you will try to get your revenge next time. Some sports clubs have the convention that the first toast is proposed by the captain of the winning side. It is then answered by his opposite number. However, in other clubs, it is always the captain of the home team who proposes the first toast. If you are representing the away team, and have been provided with refreshments, don't forget to include your thanks for these.

The staff or one's colleagues

At a firm's dinner, one of the directors may propose a toast to the staff. Also a toast may be proposed at a celebratory meal marking the completion of a particular project. In both cases the emphasis should be on the teamwork that has led to the successes described.

Wedding and other celebratory toasts

Toasts at weddings (and other family events) tend to be less formal than after-dinner toasts. You should aim to sound spontaneous and witty, but humour in bad taste should be avoided as even if the bride and groom don't mind you'll probably upset some relative or other. As with other toasts you should make a few notes of what you mean to say, and you should also make sure, at least until the toasts are over, that you do not drink too much. Another hazard of family celebrations is the airing (inadvertently or otherwise) of family grievances or battles. As with humour, if you think it is going to upset someone, leave it out.

If there is no toastmaster, the job of making sure the glasses are filled ready, then silencing the guests and announcing the toasts, is usually undertaken by the best man. The first toast is to the bride and groom, and is normally given by the bride's father, although sometimes a longstanding friend of the bride may be asked instead. The theme behind the toast, which usually lasts a few minutes, should be the good health and future happiness of the couple. The bridegroom is then expected to reply to the toast. If he does not wish to make a full speech, just a sincere 'thank you' on behalf of himself and his wife would be acceptable, but the bridegroom could also include some flattering comment about his new wife and give his thanks to both his parents and his parents-in-law who have probably done much of the work of organising the reception. The bridegroom usually finishes his reply by proposing a toast to the bridesmaids.

Traditionally, it is the best man who replies on behalf of the bridesmaids and, like everyone else, he should keep his toast short. If is often then his duty to read out the telegrams (or telemessages nowadays), and if possible he should have sorted them into order with the most important left till last, and the rude left out! It is also useful if he can enquire beforehand about family relationships so that he can add helpful details as he reads out the telegrams. For example, 'The next telegram is from Dora and Fred Jones and family, the bride's cousins in Canada' is more interesting and informative than just 'Signed Dora and Fred'. This is the standard order of events, but on less formal occasions the best man may propose the only toast 'To the bride and groom' as in the example given later in this book.

If you are asked to give the toast at other celebratory events such as christenings and coming-of-age parties, you could, if necessary, just ask the rest of the assembled company to join you in drinking a toast. However, if you can think of a relevant anecdote to tell which is not going to upset or embarrass people, this would add some sparkle to the toast. Your central theme should always be good wishes for the future.

After-dinner speeches

After-dinner speeches are something of a cross between toasts and longer talks. They usually last between 10 and 15 minutes, but do check with the organiser of the event the length of speech required. You will probably be given enough warning to have time to prepare and practise as outlined in Chapter 3, but as you will be speaking for a shorter time, it should be possible to confine your notes to a single note card.

If you are giving an after-dinner speech you should find out all you can about the likely audience, venue and programme of events. Dinner audiences can vary greatly from unresponsive, rather formal audiences to jocular noisy groups more interested in heckling than in listening to you. Having said this, the majority are likely to be fairly cheerful and friendly, and willing to listen provided your speech is not dry and boring.

The number of speeches after a dinner can also vary considerably. If there are to be several speakers, and you have any choice in the matter, you would probably do best to speak early on, before your audience has had too much time to be bored by poor speeches or to drink too much. You will, of course, need to remain sober yourself in order to deliver your speech successfully. Do remember also that, as a guest speaker, you are still 'on show' even after your speech is over.

A short speech tends to work best if you restrict yourself to one main subject area. You could then divide the subject into three main sections, and make them the main headings on your note card. If you are talking to a group who all share a common interest, such as a cricket club, do not feel your talk must include too many references to this interest: this is especially so if you know little about the subject. The club is probably bored with hearing the same old stories and quotations and may instead enjoy some comments from an outsider. Base your speech on something with which you are familiar, just keeping in mind what you know about the interests of the audience so that, wherever appropriate, you can make relevant comparisons for them. If you are invited to speak at a dinner to celebrate an anniversary, you could perhaps build your speech round interesting things that occurred around the time of the original event.

Bear in mind that after-dinner speeches are supposed to be entertaining, so do not drag in depressing information or use them as a vehicle to express a pet gripe. However, also keep in mind that you have been invited as a speaker rather than a comedian – a job which very few people can do successfully – so do not make your speech a string of loosely linked, and irrelevant jokes. You will probably want to include one or two relevant anecdotes, but bear in mind the warnings given in Chapter 3. Don't feel obliged to tell a joke in an after-dinner speech – you can be just as effective and entertaining without. A relevant joke or two could be included if you are confident that you can tell it successfully, but it is always as well to test out any jokes you intend to use on friends and relatives beforehand. They may be able to warn you that the joke is an 'old chestnut' and you are the only person not to have heard it before, or suggest that it is rather too risque. It is best to avoid 'dirty' jokes in after-dinner speaking, especially if you don't know the audience. If other speakers use dirty jokes, that is up to them, but you would probably find that much of the laughter they get is from embarrassment rather than genuine amusement. It is also unwise to try telling jokes which rely on a particular dialect or do down a particular nationality – unless, of course, you naturally speak that dialect or are of that nationality. Finally, avoid the trap of saying something like, 'Have you heard the joke about . . .'. This is almost bound to be too much of a temptation for someone in the audience to answer, 'Yes', or complete the joke for you!

It is probably more important with after-dinner speaking than with most other types of speaking to check what style of dress is appropriate. Once at the meal, it is best to eat fairly slowly and lightly in order to avoid either indigestion or a bloated feeling – neither of these are likely to help you concentrate on your speech. Also check early on the whereabouts of the toilet and washroom, and if necessary slip out before your speech to make use of the facilities. However, do let someone know that you have gone so that your speech isn't announced in your absence!

A special sort of after-dinner speech is the speech of welcome to guests. If you are asked to give such a speech remember that you are speaking on behalf of your company or society and that the speech is primarily for the guest's benefit. Avoid 'in' jokes or obscure references to people and events that will be unknown to the guests and, if you tell an anecdote, set it in context for them.

Presentations

One of the most common reasons for a presentation is because someone is leaving a job due to retirement, ill-health or a new job. Companies and societies may also present awards or diplomas to their staff or members, and such events are usually accompanied by short speeches.

If you are the person giving the speech, you could be in charge of organising the presentation, too. If so, try to choose a suitable venue for the presentation – canteens, for instance, are usually far from ideal because of offstage noises from the nearby kitchens or because their acoustics are poor. Also, consider whether it will be possible to have everyone seated or have a small platform for the presentation. Otherwise, with everyone standing at the same level, few people will be able to see what is going on. You may also need to consider the practicalities of handing over the gift or award. If it is small you can hold it until it is presented. However, do remember you will probably need to shake hands – and if the gift is bigger, things could get awkward.

Farewell speeches to someone who is leaving are usually about five to 10 minutes long. This is one of the few instances when a speech can, perhaps, be too short – an employee can feel hurt if his whole contribution to the company is summed up in about two minutes flat! Such a speech must also be sincere, so unless you are the only person who could be expected to give the speech, you would do the best not to take the job on if you have never really liked the presentee. The first point to make is that you should obviously get his name right! You will also want to praise the person and mention some of his achievements and contributions, but do avoid going 'over the top' and embarrassing everyone, as well as cheapening the value of the compliments. A bit of humour may be appropriate, and you could possibly recount an amusing incident. However, as with all such humour, the joke should be on yourself rather than the recipient of the presentation. Other points to keep in mind are to avoid dwelling too much on retirement (some people actually dread it) and to mention the person's spouse if he or she has been invited to the presentation, too. You might like to suggest that the person keeps in touch, as you would like to hear how they get on. Finally, wish them all the best in their retirement or new job, or hope for a speedy recovery, before presenting them with their gift.

A presentation of an award or diploma would probably be shorter. You should mention a little about the history of the award: for example, perhaps it is a cup which has been given every year since 1902, or a cut-glass bowl donated in memory of a past director by his wife. You will also need to detail the achievements for which it is presented and say a little about the particular contribution of the person about to receive it. All you then need to do is to congratulate the recipient, and make the presentation.

Replying to toasts and presentations
Unless you have been specifically asked to give a longer speech, replies to toasts and presentations can, and generally should, be very short. It is difficult to prepare what to say as you don't know what might be said in the toast or presentation. However, if you know you are likely to be called on to reply it might be worth jotting down a few ideas beforehand. Don't overdo the modesty in replying to toasts and presentations, and above all be sincere in your reply.

If you are asked to reply to a toast, your main task is to thank the person who proposed it and also the group who invited you to the dinner. You may be able to add some appropriate comment on something that was said in the toast, otherwise just something to the effect that you have enjoyed the event and a repeat of your thanks will suffice.

Replying to a speech and presentation is similar. Again

you should make sure you thank the person who gave the speech and the people who have given you the gift or award. You could perhaps comment on something said during the speech, otherwise a few words about how you have enjoyed your time with the firm or group and/or how you intend to make use of your retirement and the gift would be appropriate. Finish by wishing everybody all the best for the future and repeating your thanks.

School prize-givings
These are a specialised form of presentation where the actual handing over of the prizes is usually preceeded by a short speech. In order to give a successful speech at such an event, it is wise to think back to some of the disasters you probably sat through as a child and avoid some of the worst mistakes. Firstly, don't be too long-winded; 10 or 15 minutes is probably quite enough unless you have been specifically asked to speak for longer. Try to avoid talking down to or patronising the children and don't fall into the 'when I was your age' trap. Finally, watch out for possible double-meanings in your speech – children are quick to notice them and less self-controlled than adults in hiding their mirth. The unintentional use of a teacher's nickname is also a potential hazard. When you get round to handing over the prizes, you should make sure you get the recipients' names right (query any difficult ones beforehand) and offer a few words of congratulation to each of them.

Opening fêtes and bazaars
If you are asked to open such an event, you should bear in mind that the main purpose of the event is to raise funds for a particular cause rather than to listen to speeches. You should therefore be brief and to the point. There are five basic points to an opening speech: (a) welcome everyone to the event; (b) thank the organisers for all the hard work they have put in (it is usually best not to mention individual names because of the risk of upsetting those left out); (c) make a brief reference to the charity raising funds, why the funds are needed and the particular items or projects they will be used for; (d) encourage everyone to have a good time and spend plenty of money; and (e) declare the event open.

Opening buildings, laying foundation stones and planting commemorative trees

If you are asked to undertake any of these honours, you may be required to give a short speech in addition to performing the actual deed. As many of these events will be held out of doors, often in inclement weather, brevity is definitely required. After welcoming the people present, you could perhaps say a little about the history of the site (you may be able to find out what buildings used to be there from your local-studies library) and its development. Tread with care if there has been past controversy! You could follow this by a few words about the future use of the building or site. Finish by congratulating all those involved in the project and then plant the tree, cut the ribbon, lay the brick, or undertake whatever task the ceremony involves.

Open-air speaking

Speaking in the open air has its own particular problems. Unfortunately you can do little about most of them. However, if you are on a committee organising an event which will feature open-air speeches you should bear in mind the natural features of the site as well as power supplies, etc., when deciding where the speaker(s) should stand. A microphone or megaphone can help project the speakers' voices more loudly, but open-air microphones are often poorly maintained and, unless you are able to provide a good sound system, may only help some of the people to hear.

As a speaker you can improve your audibility by speaking more slowly and deliberately than usual, and by using short phrases with clear pauses between them.

Impromptu social speaking

On the whole, the best advice for beginners is probably 'don't'. If you feel you have made a mess of it your confidence will be dented and you may be put off public speaking for good. However, if there is no way out, the next best advice is to keep what you say short and sincere. You should let what you say arise from the occasion. For example at a family gathering you could express your enjoyment of the event and thank the person who organised it. You could maybe also include a short (but not too embarrassing) anecdote concerning the person or persons for whom the event is being held. At a dinner given by a society, in addition to expressing your enjoyment and thanks, you could perhaps think of something to say concerning your links with the group.

Longer, informative talks

This section is fairly brief, because a longer talk was used as the main example in Chapters 3 and 4. The other talks described here all share a common aim to inform, and in some cases also to teach. These aims need not exclude a certain amount of entertainment, too, though reports should stick strictly to the facts.

Talks to local societies, luncheon clubs, etc

This type of talking is covered in some detail in Chapters 3 and 4. Talks to local societies are usually evening events, with the speaker talking for about 30 to 45 minutes followed by a question time of 10 to 15 minutes. Because of the time constraints of lunch breaks, talks to luncheon clubs are generally shorter, perhaps 15 to 30 minutes plus a short question time, and you certainly must not overrun and throw everyone's afternoon schedules. Luncheon clubs may consist of people with a common interest or profession but some are purely social groups with a wide cross-section of people.

Evening classes and lecturing

Although these types of public speaking may be very similar to giving a talk, you should keep in mind that people are attending because they want to learn. Having said this, however, you want your audience to continue coming to your talks and a certain amount of entertainment will help maintain attendances as well as often making the information easier to assimilate. If you are not sure at what level to pitch your talk, you can generally keep everyone happy by 'tactful education'. This involves using phrases like 'as you all probably know' with some fact you feel they ought to know. Probably they don't, but such phrases can help to ensure that all the basic points are understood before you go on to more complex matters. Sometimes people are asked to lecture because of their knowledge and expertise rather than because of their public speaking ability. If you are one of these people and feel very nervous, it may be better to use fairly full notes rather than give a garbled and incomprehensible talk. However, if you can manage with notes on cards as outlined in Chapter 3, your talk will probably be much more pleasant to listen to. Visual aids are fairly important in this kind of talking and you should keep in mind all the points made about relevance, readability and use of specimens.

Talks during a conference or seminar
Talking fairly late on in a conference has both advantages and disadvantages. By listening to other speakers and watching the audience you should be able to get some idea of the general mood and with that clues about the best way to present your own talk. However, towards the end of a series of talks the audience is usually more tired and restless, so you may find you need to make your talk more lively and spontaneous in order to retain their interest. If you are following other speakers, do try to note down a few points on which you can comment during your talk, as this will help to give overall continuity to the event.

Presenting a report at work
In some ways it may be more difficult to speak before colleagues at work than to strangers, as you will have to face your colleagues the following day, and they may not show you the same respect that they would give to strangers. You will probably have most of the facts you need for such a report at your fingertips and you may find your main problem is deciding what to leave out. The length and content of your report will probably be dictated by what you have been asked to do. However, in most cases, your main aim should be to state the facts clearly and concisely. Anecdotes or displays of great eloquence are not usually expected or wanted and so you may be able to use full notes or even read out your report. As you will probably be asked to answer questions afterwards, you will need more information available than you actually include in your report, and you should of course, check and double-check all the facts for accuracy.

Graphs and other diagrams are often useful to present

certain types of facts, but if you are going to point to just one copy do make sure first of all that it is big enough for everyone to see. It must also be well presented. Alternatively you could produce photocopies of your diagrams and provide a copy for each person present. In this case, though, do make sure that copies are clearly labelled so that everyone can easily lay their hands on 'Figure 3' or whatever when you refer to it. If your report is one of a series or you are to be called in for just part of a meeting, make arrangements to set up any visual aids before the start if feasible. Otherwise ask people to bear with you and don't rush into your report before everything is set up properly or all the papers are distributed.

Presenting other reports
In your capacity as chairman, secretary or treasurer of a society, you may be asked to present a report to the group. Such a report is usually purely factual and should just deal with the main features of the period in question. For example the chairman of a charity speaking at the Annual General Meeting would probably outline the achievements of the past year. He might add a little about how he sees things going in the future and finish by thanking everyone for their support during the year. It is quite acceptable to read such a report, but do bear in mind audibility and talk to the group rather than reading down to your papers.

The technique for presenting a report to other organisations such as trades unions or political groups is basically the same – though you will probably have a rather larger audience.

Persuasive speaking
Speaking at public and political meetings, and to the press, has been left until last because it is probably the most difficult type of public speaking, best avoided until you are reasonably experienced. In contrast to most audiences, who are generally friendly and forgiving, audiences at such meetings can be openly hostile. If you are giving this type of speech you must always keep in mind that your overriding aim is to persuade people and to achieve support. Your speech should build up to a climax at which you tell the

audience what you want them to do. If your speech builds up to a climax earlier than you had intended, it is better to shut up and sit down at that point, rather than ramble on to an anticlimax.

Even if your speech is not specifically to the press, political and public meetings are often reported in the newspapers. It may therefore be useful to have copies of your speech available for any journalists present to help them to report what you say accurately.

Public meetings and debates

Debates, of the kind held by debating societies, are a slightly ritualised form of meeting, where the points of view are often argued for their own sake in order to provide experience in presenting and successfully defending a case. A public meeting may be called whenever there is a contentious point – for example, villagers may call one to discuss views about a controversial road scheme. In both public meetings and debates, there will probably be guidelines as to how long an individual speech should be, either set down in the rules or announced by the chairman before the main business of the meeting.

If the chairman is efficient he will make sure that speakers keep to the guidelines. So, in this kind of speaking you must always keep an eye on the time to avoid being stopped before you have put your final and strongest point. Whatever your case, you should state your views clearly and concisely. You must, of course, make sure all your facts are correct and indisputable. It is sensible to give prominence to strong points supporting your case, and only mention those opposing points which can easily be demolished and shown up as false or misguided. However, you should know the opposition's case well, since this will help to strengthen your arguments and enable you to deal with difficult questions. Do not be tempted to overstate your case, however, as this may weaken your argument if shown up. Try to avoid saying anything that may provoke awkward questions or facetious remarks. Finally, remember that you are more likely to encourage the audience to support your views if they feel personally involved. If possible give examples which relate directly to them. They will also feel more involved if you use the form 'we' rather than 'you' wherever possible: what you are endeavouring to do is to create a feeling of 'all of us fighting a common enemy'.

Political meetings
These are similar in many ways to public meetings except that people will be arguing in support of a particular political party and its views. You can learn much about the techniques of political speaking by watching successful politicians in action on television or in person. Many politicians make use of the power of repetition and easily remembered catch phrases. Politicians also make use of group psychology. With a large audience it is often possible to generate a group feeling – people become carried away with the general feeling of the mass and then the whole audience acts as one. As with other persuasive speaking you should, of course, deliberately concentrate on your strong points. You should also aim to finish any speech on a high and confident note.

A favourite ploy which politicians in particular use to great effect is to make three separate points about an issue, each helping to build up to a final climax. For instance, a politician may say of another political party, 'Not only is the X party devoid of new ideas on how to revive the economy, it has never in the past offered any constructive ideas on how to revive the economy, and furthermore it has never looked *likely* to offer any ideas on how to revive the economy.'

Rallies and demonstrations
This is a special kind of persuasive speaking and, as such events are usually outside, you should bear in mind the necessity to speak clearly and use short phrases. Repetition and group psychology work well here, too, but as the people at a rally will usually be those already committed to the cause your speech would probably dwell on the practicalities of what the group could and should do to further its cause.

Sales presentations
A sales presentation is something of a cross between a report and speaking to a political group or a public meeting. Your main aim, which must always be kept in mind, is to *sell* the goods or ideas in question. You will need to state the

arguments for buying or using the items, or for taking on your company to do the work needed. These arguments can then be developed with supporting facts, and you should, of course, finish with a firm conclusion or a good summing up. Impeccable presentation, both of your talk, and any visual aids you may use, is vital.

Dealing with hecklers and awkward questions

In most types of public speaking, a good chairman will probably protect you from unfair questioning. However, in persuasive speaking, you will be expected to face your critics, and much of your credibility will depend on how you cope with them. At times, hecklers and people putting awkward questions can even help you to make your point more successfully, and they will certainly keep you on your toes.

The way you deal with such problems depends mainly on your personality. However, one thing you should never do is lose your temper. With a small audience, you may be able to deal with the point made by the heckler on the spot, but this should only be done if you can answer the point briefly, without interrupting the main flow of your speech. Otherwise you can ask the heckler to be kind enough to let you complete what you are saying without interruption and to put his point later on at question time. If you have the experience and are good at quick repartee, you may be able to reply in a suitably brief and amusing fashion. However, do try to avoid saying anything you may regret afterwards. If the shock of an apt reply does not silence your heckler, don't let the meeting degenerate into a slanging match between the two of you. Should none of these techniques work, all you can do is to carry on regardless, or ask the chairman to have the heckler removed.

Some techniques for dealing with awkward or aggressive questioning have already been dealt with in Chapter 4, but don't automatically assume that all questions are aggressive. It may just be that the questioner's nerves make it sound that way. Do try to answer all questions; audiences are quick to spot evasive techniques and interpret them as meaning you don't have an acceptable answer. If you don't know the answer to a question, the wisest course may be to say so.

Dealing with the press

Press conferences
It is outside the scope of this book to deal with the organisation of press conferences or, indeed, discuss whether or not
they are the best form of publicity for a particular purpose.
However, if you are asked to speak at such a conference
you should remember that the main aim is to accurately put
across your message. On the whole, column-inches matter
less than an accurate picture in the newspapers.

You will probably be given some guidance on the length
of the speech required, but generally, at press conferences,
the most successful speeches are short and simple. Choose
your words carefully – something that works well in a speech
may not sound so good when written in a newspaper. Try to
put yourself in a journalist's shoes and consider what is
likely to make a good story. Also keep in mind the differing
needs of local and national newspapers, and the general
and specialist journals. However, don't try to tell the journalists how they should report your speech – it is their job to
determine that.

Reports in the press can be much more accurate if you
provide handouts listing relevant names and positions, facts
and figures, and any technical details, or even a copy of the
complete speech. Let the journalists know early on that
these press packs will be available after the conference.
During your speech they can concentrate on noting down
the gist of what you are saying rather than trying to get
names and other details.

Either you, or the person chairing the conference, will
probably invite questions afterwards, and all questions should
be dealt with courteously and equally, whatever your personal feelings about any particular journalist or his paper.
After the main business, mingle and be friendly and deal
with any other questions that may come up, but try not to be
caught off guard in this less formal atmosphere.

Press interviews
If you are involved in something newsworthy you may be
telephoned by a journalist and asked to answer a few
questions over the telephone.If you are tackled on a difficult
subject and feel you need a little time to prepare your

statements and arguments you can always stall for time by claiming you have someone with you or are in the middle of a meeting and offering to 'phone back shortly'. Or if your call is taken by someone else you could ask them to make an excuse for you. But don't overdo this or you may get a reputation for evasiveness!

Before you start to give an interview to a journalist try to get an idea of how long an interview he wants and what line he is proposing to take. Choose the words of your answers carefully. Nearly all journalists follow a strict code of conduct because they have their own reputations to protect and because they wish to retain the goodwill of the people who are likely to be future sources. They will probably record what you say by shorthand or on a tape recorder and can therefore accurately quote your words. What you must watch out for, however, are statements that could be mis-construed if taken out of context. Tell the journalist if some-thing you say is strictly off the record. Most journalists will respect your wishes if they are backed by sound reasons, but are under no obligation to do so if they genuinely feel that it is in the public's best interests to hear such information.

6. Radio and Television

Today, television and radio are more open to public participation than ever before. Therefore, many more people than in the past are likely to find themselves taking part in a broadcast at some stage of their life. As well as being asked to give a talk or an interview, people can contribute to 'phone-in' programmes and discussions.

Probably the most important technique for contributing successfully to either television or radio is to forget the millions who may be listening to the programme and concentrate instead on the person to whom you are talking. If you are being interviewed this would obviously be the interviewer who is, after all, acting as the representative of the audience. If you are recording a talk in a studio you should imagine you are talking to just one person and speak specifically to them. That way each individual listening at home will feel that *he* is the one to whom you are talking. Another important point to remember about radio and television is that they are immediate and topical media, where split-second timing is important to keep to the published programme. Finally, if you have sufficient warning before taking part in a broadcast, do listen or watch the programme to which you will be contributing so that you are familiar with its style.

Radio

Radio broadcasts may be either pre-recorded or 'live'. The recording will usually take place in a studio, but may also be made outside in the street or in someone's home or work place.

Many people listening to the radio are doing something

else as well, such as washing the dishes or driving the car. This means that you may have to work hard to get, and keep, their attention. Also, because they may not be concentrating fully, they may hear what they expect to hear rather than what you actually say. Unlike a 'live' audience, they are unable to ask you to repeat or explain any points after your talk. You must therefore take particular care to be clear and articulate. In contrast to television, only your voice is available to put over an image, so the more expression you can put into what you say, the better. However, because there is no visual image to distract the audience, any attempts at a false or unnatural voice, as well as any accidental noises such as knocking a microphone or coughing, will be more obvious.

Television
In television broadcasts, you will be both seen *and* heard and you should try to make sure that your visual and sound images do not contradict one another. Because you will be seen, many of the points mentioned in the chapters about appearing before a live audience apply here. Your clothing should be tidy, appropriate and comfortable. Unless it is an integral part of your style, avoid large or copious and distracting jewellery. Also remember that certain striped fabrics produce interference patterns on television so avoid these, too, if you can. Ask the producer for advice if necessary. You will probably be told to ignore the camera, but in your eagerness to avoid it try not to constantly shift your gaze everywhere else. Try not to fidget. If your legs will be seen by the camera try to sit in a relaxed position with your legs out in front of you rather than crossed or wrapped round the chair. To avoid embarrassment ladies in short skirts should also beware of camera angles, especially when seated on a platform.

Studios and rehearsals

Television studios, in particular, can be quite daunting places if they are unfamiliar. There will probably be a number of people dashing around doing their jobs and they may not realise that it is all new to you. If possible, you should let the production team know that you are new to broadcasting and ask them to help you. Most broadcasters are friendly and will be willing to explain things as far as time allows. In studios, you may come across three types of microphone. Boom microphones are usually suspended above the conversation and with these you should just speak normally and ignore any movements they may make. In radio broadcasting you may have a microphone on a table in front of you. This will probably be able to pick up sounds from any direction. As it is sensitive, do avoid hitting it. Today, miniature microphones are commonly used. These are clipped on to clothing or hung round your neck. This type of microphone allows much more freedom of movement than fixed microphones.

When you arrive at the studio, the technicians will probably need to carry out final checks on equipment and work out camera and microphone positions. If you are asked to give a voice test, say something realistic. However, avoid 'dry runs' of your script. This is because if you rehearse a script in the studio, there is a danger that during the broadcast itself, you will concentrate too hard on trying to remember what sounded good before: instead, you should think only of what you are doing *now*. As with all other public speaking engagements, you should treat any drinks you may be offered beforehand with a degree of caution.

During the recording itself, try to ignore what is happening elsewhere in the studio and control room. In a television studio there will be a floor manager who is coordinating everyone involved and he will be the person to communicate with.

If you are pre-recorded, it is best not to ask for a playback. Very few people are likely to be entirely happy with the recording; however, re-recordings can be much worse. If the recording is not live what you have said will almost certainly be edited. The broadcasters themselves want a good programme to enhance their own reputations, so they will be interested in improving it, too. However, if during the recording they suggest a restart, you can assume there are good reasons, so it is best to agree.

Talks

You are more likely to be asked to give a radio talk then a talk for television, as talks tend to lack the visual appeal required by television. In many ways the preparation needed for a radio talk is similar to that for a talk before a live audience, but there are certain basic differences.

Firstly, remember the importance of timing. If your radio talk is longer than required, your audience will not be able to bear with you for a few more minutes. Instead, your talk will have to be edited down, maybe missing out points that you thought were quite important. So time your talk carefully. Different people obviously talk at different rates, but 120-130 words per minute is a fairly average speed. From this you can calculate how much to write.

Also, remember the point made earlier – that many people listening to the radio are only giving a part of their concentration to it. You will therefore have to make sure you speak clearly. Also, the sentences you use should be well phrased so that the information needed to understand the rest of the sentence is given first. When broadcasting, you will be getting no audience feedback to tell you how your talk is being received. So you would do best to steer clear of most kinds of humour.

Otherwise, like any other talk, your radio talk should have a logical framework including an introduction, a main body and a conclusion. It should be written out as you would speak using 'I'd' rather than 'I would', etc., and should include whatever punctuation you find most helpful.

If you are giving a radio talk, you will need to use a full script rather than note cards so that you keep accurately to the planned length. However, practice is still necessary so that you get your pauses and emphases correct and do not stumble over any awkward pronunciations. Try to visualise what you are saying as you say it, and even gesticulate if it helps, as this will inject more life and emphasis into your voice. You will probably be asked to submit a copy of your script to the radio station beforehand, and they may well suggest some improvements. On your own copy of the script you might find it useful to mark timings so that you know how far through the script you should be after a certain time. You could also use your own system of underlining, colours, etc., to mark up emphasis and key words. (If you give a talk on television your script may be transcribed on to an auto-cue system. Here the script appears just above the camera, enabling you to read it while still looking at the camera.)

When you arrive at the recording studio you will probably be asked to read your talk aloud so that the timing can be checked and the equipment adjusted for your voice level. If you are in a studio on your own you will probably be provided with feedback headphones so that the studio manager can give you instructions and advice.

Interviews

Preparation

There are any number of reasons why you may be asked to take part in an interview on radio or television. You may be asked because you are the chairman or spokesman for a firm which has just landed a new deal or because you are an acknowledged expert on a certain subject which has just hit the news. Your local radio station may wish to do an interview with a representative of a local society, or you may just be a likely looking person approached on the street! Interviews can be either friendly or challenging and may be live or recorded. In some cases (for example most interviews with scientists in which they explain their subject to the general public) the interview may be scripted. In other cases you will have to come up with your answers on the spot and without preparation.

You may be given very short notice before an interview. Remember that you can always refuse. However, you may have to balance the effects of giving a poor and unconvincing interview against the reaction to, 'A spokesman for X firm declined to comment.' If, as a representative of a local group, you refuse an interview you may not be asked again and you may lose a chance of valuable publicity for your group.

However short the notice, try to find out as much as you can about what is required. You will want to know the following:

Will the interview be live or pre-recorded? Pre-recorded interviews are less nerve-racking but will almost certainly be cut and edited. Producers must follow a code of ethics and should not intentionally tamper with the meaning of what you say, but they may cut something that you personally thought was important. However, to balance this they will also cut errors and any possibly impolite remarks during the editing and this will improve how you sound.

Will the interview be supporting or attacking your point of view? If the intention is to attack your views you may not be told this in so many words but you will probably be able to tell from any evasive answers you receive. It is also worth checking that the radio or television station has a correct impression of your viewpoint, as it has been known for an interviewee to express the opposite view from that expected because of a misunderstanding somewhere along the line.

Who will be conducting the interview? This may give you some clues as to the way the interview will be handled. However, remember that interviewers, like chairmen, should treat all sides equally whatever their personal views. Their job as interviewers is to speak on behalf of the general public and to ask the questions the public want answered. They may themselves not be personally biased, but perhaps feel that by expressing views opposite to your own they may stimulate a more revealing answer.

How long will the interview last? If it is to be very short you will have to be particularly careful to get any important points over early on before the interview is finished.

When and where will the interview take place? If it is at a studio make sure you have adequate instructions to find it, and if it is to be recorded at your home or work place arrange to be left alone and undisturbed. Don't allow friends or colleagues to 'sit in' on the interview – they are only likely to distract you.

Will you be provided with a list of questions in advance, or at least have an opportunity of discussing the outlines of the interview? It is not unreasonable to ask for this.

Again, however short the notice, do as much preparation as you can. You will need to arm yourself with the facts and figures you may need and it would be useful to note on cards the main points you wish to make. If you use any cards on television you should, of course, use them discreetly. As with other forms of public speaking, it is usually best to concentrate on a couple of important points and make sure you put these over successfully. If you make a large number of points they can easily be forgotten by listeners. However, exactly what you will say will, of course, be governed by the questions. As in most interviews, time is of the essence, so you would also do well to try to think of short and concise ways of putting over your points. If you don't know the questions in advance, it may help your confidence to think of the worst question you might be asked and work out an answer to it.

The interview itself
Allow plenty of time to get yourself to a recording studio. Studios are often difficult to find and your voice and poise is unlikely to be improved by running up numerous flights of stairs when you discover, a few minutes before recording time, that you should be in room X (at the top of the building) rather than room Y in the basement.

At the studio you will probably meet the producer and the interviewer (or in a remote studio you will be linked through to them by telephone, radio or video connections). If you are new to interviews and broadcasting, do tell the broadcasters this and put yourself in their hands. They want to get the best from you and will usually be friendly.

Before the recording you may run through the questions with the interviewer. The technician will also need to make last-minute checks on their equipment. If you are being interviewed on television, the make-up department will apply whatever cosmetics are needed to make your face suitable for televising.

As stressed earlier, during the actual recording, you should put out of your mind the audience sitting at home, and concentrate instead on the interviewer. (But be aware that an experienced interviewer could use this apparent intimacy to draw from you statements, opinions or anecdotes that you would rather keep out of the public domain.) Listen carefully to the interviewer's questions and, unless you are deliberately trying to hide something, answer the question as put. Remember the time constraints and get your most important points over first, before the interviewer has to cut in with another question or the interview is brought to a close. However, in your attempts to be brief, try not to go to the other extreme; answering 'Yes' or 'No' to all questions does not produce a very satisfactory interview. Unless you are deliberately stalling for time don't waste time by repeating the interviewer's question or commenting, 'That's a very good question'. Also use short and straightforward phrases wherever possible – for example, 'I believe . . .' says exactly the same as 'I, personally, am of the opinion . . .' and does it in far fewer words. If you are a person who easily picks up voice tones and accents, try to make sure that your voice does not start to mimic the tone of the interviewer: it may sound as if you are mocking him. Finally, remember that the interviewer cannot force an answer from you, although he can make it obvious to the audience if he thinks you are being deliberately evasive.

Discussion programmes

Discussion programmes are often made up of a core of experienced broadcasters who can be relied upon to perform well. Other people may be invited to take part because they are known to hold certain views, or because they have done something newsworthy. A discussion group will always have some kind of controller or chairman, whose job is to make sure that everyone is given a chance to have their say and to encourage the less forthcoming speakers. Many features will be similar to those described for interviews and, as with interviews, you should find out as much as you can beforehand about the programme. In particular, you will want to know who will be chairing the discussion and who the other participants are likely to be.

7. The Role of the Chairman

In order for any kind of official event, such as a meeting or a dinner, to run smoothly, there must be someone in charge. This person is usually known as the chairman, though sometimes a president fulfils a similar function. Even entertainment events need someone in charge, and the role played by a compére has many similarities to that of the chairman of a meeting. Because there must always be someone to take charge of a meeting or similar event, it is important to appoint a vice-chairman who can deputise for the chairman in his absence.

The duties of a chairman are basically to control and guide the meeting or event in an unobtrusive manner. He should know how the event is to be run and should follow the rules determined by the group as well as any rules of law and common courtesy. If there are arguments as to how the event should proceed, he is the one who will have to make the final decision. He may also need to interpret the procedures so that everyone knows and understands what should happen. A chairman should also see that everyone is fairly and impartially treated, that the event runs to its agreed schedule, that people do not disgress from the business in hand, and that interruptions are kept to a minimum. Finally, he is the one in command if there is any emergency – for example if a fire breaks out he should make sure everyone vacates the premises in a quick but orderly fashion, and that the emergency services are called.

In order to fulfil these duties satisfactorily, a chairman needs certain personal qualities. Although he obviously needs to speak reasonably fluently and is not bashful about addressing groups of people, the qualities needed are not exactly the same as those for most other types of public speaking. In fact, some people who are good public speakers in other circumstances may be too extrovert or fond of the sound of their own voice to make ideal chairmen. Probably the most important quality that a chairman should possess is decisiveness. This doesn't mean that he should impose his views on the group or bully people in any way, in fact quite the opposite, but he should be willing to take the lead as required and, having made a decision, stick to it. A good chairman also needs to be a tactful person, able to deal with all sorts of people (including the awkward!) in a firm but courteous way. He must also be approachable by everyone and they must be confident that he will deal with the matters in hand in a fair and impartial way. Finally, he needs to be a reasonably calm and placid person in order that he can deal with whatever happens without 'losing his cool'.

Unfortunately, chairmen are not always chosen solely on the basis of their personal qualities. Common reasons for nominations are because the person in question can be relied upon to speak without shyness, because it would be diplomatic to do so, or simply because no-one else will take on the job. However, most people are capable of being a reasonable chairman, though they may need to devote some effort to cultivating the necessary qualities.

Having dealt with chairing in very general terms, the remainder of this chapter deals with the special features of chairing various types of events.

Chairing dinners

If you are asked to chair a dinner you are, in a sense, acting as the host on behalf of the group. Your duties, as with any other chairing, are to make sure things run smoothly and that everyone, and in particular any special guests, are kept happy. You may have to deal with any unduly rowdy behaviour or any emergency that may occur and, if you do not have a toastmaster, you will probably be expected to take on that duty, too. You must remember that your job is to be in control, but unobtrusively; you should not aim to be the star performer or to outshine the guests in any way.

Other people may undertake much of the preparatory work, such as preparing the toast list, before a dinner. However, as chairman you are nominally in charge so you should check that all the necessary arrangements have been made.

On the day itself, you should arrive early so that you can check all the arrangements at the venue and also so that you can welcome the guests. Pay particular attention to any special guests and make sure that their needs are met. Confirm the details of the programme with them, and make sure you have all the details you need to introduce their speeches.

In addition to welcoming the guests, you will also need to liaise with the caterers. A few minutes before the meal is due to be served, you or the toastmaster should make an announcement asking everyone to move towards the tables. This is usually quite a slow process and you may need to ask people again or get some of the other officials to make a move in the hope that others will follow. Once everyone is assembled at the tables, you or the toastmaster may then knock for silence so that grace can be said. This may be said by a chaplain or clergyman if one is present or by the chairman himself. However, if you as chairman are acting as toastmaster it may be best to ask someone else to perform this duty. If grace is not said, the chairman should wait until everyone is stood in place. If he then indicates to the guests and officials to sit down, everyone else should follow.

During the meal itself, as long as there are no emergencies, you are then free to relax a little and enjoy the food, though you will probably be sitting next to the special guests and you should of course engage them in conversation.

At the end of the meal, your official duties start again with the announcement of the toasts and any after-dinner speeches. The Loyal Toast is traditionally proposed soon after the final course has been cleared away, and before the coffee. It is usually proposed by the chairman, though again if you are acting as toastmaster as well you may ask someone else to propose it. There is often then a short break before any other toasts are proposed. If you are acting as toastmaster, your duty is to knock for silence, and then introduce each toast by words along the lines of, 'Ladies and Gentlemen, I have great pleasure in calling on Mr X to propose (or reply to) the toast of. . . .' If you yourself are to propose or reply to any of the toasts you should ask one of the other officials to call for that particular toast or reply. After-dinner speeches should be announced in a similar fashion. Finally, at the end of the dinner you will need to say a few words to round the event off. Something along the lines of, 'Well, Ladies and Gentlemen, it has been a very successful and enjoyable evening and I am sure we all regret it has to come to an end so quickly' might be suitable, but there are many other ways you can bring the dinner to a conclusion.

Chairing meetings with guest speakers

Your duties as chairman of a meeting with a guest speaker are to smooth the way for both the speaker and the audience so that the meeting is an enjoyable and worthwhile occasion for all concerned. You may not be the person who makes all the preparatory arrangements, but you should make sure everything necessary has been done before the meeting. The list given at the beginning of Chapter 3 details the arrangements that will need to be discussed with the speaker. You will also need to make sure that suitable room has been booked, that any refreshments have been organised, and that the talk is publicised as appropriate. Also, remember to buttonhole someone to propose the vote of thanks after the talk.

On the day of the talk itself, you should arrive early to check arrangements at the venue and to be on hand to deal with any last-minute problems that may arise. Check that the seating arrangements seem satisfactory and that any tables or lecterns promised are there. Make sure the lighting and heating are suitable, and finally check that a supply of water has been provided for the speaker. Welcome the speaker when he arrives and don't forget that he may be feeling rather nervous and may need all the encouragement and help you can give. The speaker may have equipment to set up, and you or a colleague should be on hand to help as required. Before you both take your places in front of the audience, confirm with the speaker the length of his talk, and ask for any information you need to do the introduction. Also check whether he wants some kind of discreet warning a few minutes before his time is up.

You should, of course, start the meeting on time, and if

there is any society business to be dealt with this should not extend into the time allotted to the speaker. If the business is very short you may perhaps invite the speaker to sit in on the meeting (if there is nothing confidential to be discussed). Otherwise, he should be entertained in a nearby room by a member of the group who does not need to be present for the business. If you hold a longer business meeting before your talks, it may be best to follow the business by a break for refreshments. The speaker can then arrive and get his equipment set up during the break.

The points you should mention when introducing a speaker are covered in more detail in Chapter 5, but in summary, you should include his name (and who, if anyone, he represents), his qualifications for speaking on the subject, and the title of his talk.

During the talk you will normally stay seated beside the speaker and you should be ready to help him with any equipment if necessary. Try to look as interested and attentive as you can, even if his talk does turn out to be extremely boring! Interruptions are less likely at a talk than during a business meeting, but if any of the audience do start to whisper among themselves or cause any other kind of disturbance, you should signal to them to be quiet.

Once the talk has finished, and the applause has died down you are in the limelight again. Providing the speaker has agreed to take questions you should now announce this. In a small meeting the question time would probably be quite informal, but in other meetings you might also announce that questioners should raise their hand for attention, and that when putting their questions they should stand and address the chair. If there are likely to be many questions you might also stress the need for brevity and point out that you will only accept one question (perhaps plus a supplementary one) from each questioner – at least until everyone else who wants to ask a question has done so. You are equally likely to be faced with the opposite problem though – a general reluctance to put questions. You should be prepared for this and have a question of your own ready. Alternatively, before the meeting, you could ask one or two friends in the audience to ask questions to get the session going. In any case, give encouraging looks to potential questioners who may, perhaps, be a bit diffident about putting their questions.

During question time, look around the whole audience so that you do not miss questioners. It is often useful to repeat questions so that both the speaker and all the audience know exactly what was asked. However, do not do this without consulting the speaker first; some speakers do not like this practice because potentially it allows the chairman to put his own interpretation or emphasis into the question. You may also need to 'translate' local dialect or accents for the speaker, or provide relevant local information to explain the reasoning behind the question. You should also help disentangle complicated questions if necessary. Sometimes questioners may attempt to use a question just to put over their own views or even to give a speech. If this happens you may be justified in pointing out that the 'question' was not really relevant, or you could ask the person to conclude his question in order to give others time to ask questions. Finally, you should deal firmly with any grossly unfair or insulting questions. Give warning when the time allotted for questions is almost up by announcing that you will take only one or two further questions.

At the end of the meeting, thank the speaker briefly and sincerely, and make sure that he is offered refreshment, given a lift to the station if required, etc. Finally, make sure that someone writes to thank him for his talk.

Chairing meetings

Because the duties of the chairman of a general business meeting, a public meeting or a committee have many similarities, the details given below are generalised to apply to any of them. The special features of different types of meetings are dealt with in the following chapter, and terms that are defined there are indicated in capitals below.

Before the meeting you should make sure that all the necessary arrangements are made. If the meeting is a regular occurrence, the procedures for who does what will probably be based on precedent. However, if it is a one-off meeting or the first meeting of a new organisation you may need to call a preliminary 'committee' meeting to discuss arrangements and allocate responsibilities. As well as drawing up an AGENDA, and making arrangements for the venue, equipment, etc., you will also need to ensure that adequate publicity is given before the meeting and that any regulations concerning statutory NOTICE of the meeting are complied with.

As chairman, you should arrive early at the meeting so that you can check that all arrangements have been made satisfactorily and deal with any last-minute problems.

You must start the meeting on time (but not early!), and your first duty is to make sure that the meeting has been convened correctly and that any rules concerning a QUORUM are met. That being done, you declare the meeting open. You should first state the reason for the meeting. That may sometimes seem a little superfluous, but it does not help to fix in everyone's minds why they are there. It may also help you if, later on, you need to deal with people who are side-tracking or bringing in irrelevant points. You should also say who you are if anyone present may not know and, if appropriate, should introduce any guests and newcomers. Finally, you should state any details of how the meeting is to be run. This is particularly important if these details differ from previous meetings or if there are newcomers who may not know the procedures followed. For example, you might define time limits for speakers during a debate, or might remind people that all remarks should be addressed to the chair and that speakers should stand and keep their remarks brief and relevant.

In many meetings there are then standard items in the agenda. MINUTES OF THE PREVIOUS MEETING and MATTERS ARISING are two such items which are usually dealt with before the main business of the meeting.

During a meeting, the chairman's role is to keep the meeting going as smoothly as possible, and to make sure it is fairly conducted. He should also endeavour to ensure that the agreed agenda is followed, and that the meeting finishes on time. He will need to make sure that all the rules and regulations (defined in a rulebook or before the meeting) are adhered to, and if there is any dispute as to their interpretation he will have to define the interpretation to be accepted. For this reason, a chairman must familiarise himself with any such rules and regulations, though he may well refer to the SECRETARY of the organisation for clarification of some of the finer details. If others in the meeting feel that the chairman has overlooked a departure from the rules they can point this out to him by bringing up a POINT OF ORDER. The chairman may also need to deal with people who are side-tracking from the business in hand or who are speaking for longer than they should. In both these cases great tact is needed to avoid offence, but the job is made much easier if the exact business and time limits have been defined earlier. A chairman must be firm, and it is much better to risk upsetting one person, than to risk upsetting the whole meeting by not being in control. If someone is over-running their allotted time, the best course is to interrupt and ask them to bring what they are saying to a close. They should then be allowed to complete just that point but no more. In a formal debate, a CLOSURE motion might be proposed.

Courteous calm is usually the best technique to deal with any undue disturbances or rudeness. The person(s) in question should be brought to order in as tactful a way as possible, but you should make it clear that you do not intend to tolerate such behaviour. If the problems persist there are various courses of action open to you. The best course may be to ADJOURN THE MEETING for a fixed period of time (15 minutes or so may be adequate), during which time you hope feelings may calm down a little and the person(s) may be persuaded to see some sense and behave more rationally. If things get really bad you can always adjourn the meeting until another day, or even close it altogether but this fairly drastic course should be avoided if possible. The alternative course of action is to threaten to remove from the meeting the person or persons causing the problem, but this threat should only be made if you have the ways and means to follow it through if necessary.

Another important duty of a chairman is to keep a balance between diverse views. He must make sure that all are fairly treated and that everyone who wishes to put their views (and is entitled to) gets an opportunity. He may have his own views on the subject, and may give them if requested, but he must not let these influence the way the meeting is conducted. In other words he must act impartially. If the members of the meeting feel that the chairman is not acting impartially, and perhaps not giving someone a fair say, they can carry a MOTION that 'Mr X be heard', and the chairman will have to bow to the meeting's wishes.

When all the items on the agenda have been dealt with, or time constraints bring the meeting to an end, the chairman must then close the meeting. In some cases he may need to summarize the decisions of the meeting and allocate duties in order to make sure that someone is dealing with all the actions needed. Her should normally announce the date and place of the next meeting, thank everyone for attending, then declare the meeting closed. Once this has been done, no further business may officially be conducted.

Chairing conferences and similar events

The chairman at a conference should be the person who always knows what is going on. He will probably have delegated many of the arrangements prior to the conference, but should keep closely in touch with the other organisers. He should, of course, arrive at the venue early. During the conference itself he should also delegate wherever possible (for example, he could ask others to chair individual sessions), but he must retain overall control and act as linkman. He is usually the person who makes general announcements to the whole conference; for example if there are any room or timetable changes. He would also probably be the appropriate person to chair any summing-up sessions. The chairman should be on hand to deal with any problems during the conference and he must be good at making quick decisions and speaking off the cuff, as he will not know beforehand how events may turn out. It is hard work chairing a conference as you are always 'on duty', even during the evening when everyone else may be relaxing over drinks. However, it can also be very satisfying if everything proceeds reasonably close to plans!

Compéring

Most entertainment events need someone to be in control and to act as link-man. If you are asked to undertake such a role, your function is to introduce the acts, and to try to keep the audience happy if there are any holdups or other problems. You must remember that the audience are there for the entertainment, not to listen to you, so your introductions should be brief and to the point. You should not try to be funny, especially if you are introducing a 'real' comedian, though you may need to use a humorous anecdote or two to keep the audience amused if you have to fill a gap while backstage problems are dealt with. However, if there is a major delay it is better to just go on stage and explain the problems to the audience and then suggest they talk amongst themselves for a while. You could add an assurance that the act will be well worth waiting for. If necessary you may need to appear again to give a progress report, but you should not continually pop on and off the stage like a jack-in-the-box.

8. Meetings

This chapter attempts to define some of the commonly used terms connected with meetings. Obviously, all organisations will differ in the way they run meetings, but there are many basic similarities which are outlined here. The definitions given are intended to help new chairmen (as well as other officials and members of groups) understand the ways in which meetings are run, and are *not* intended as legal definitions. The terms are arranged in groups, and terms defined elsewhere in the chapter are indicated in capitals.

Personnel

This section deals only with duties connected with meetings. The officials usually have additional duties.

The CONVENOR is the person who calls a meeting. He sends out the NOTICE and AGENDA and oversees the arrangements for the meetings, such as booking a room, tidying up afterwards, etc. The convenor's duties are often shared by the CHAIRMAN and SECRETARY of an existing group. If a new organisation is being set up, the convenor is the person who coordinates the arrangements for the first meeting. Once this meeting has elected a chairman he will then take control.

The CHAIRMAN is the person who controls a meeting. His duties are described in Chapter 7. The VICE-CHAIRMAN (or deputy chairman) deputises for the Chairman in his absence. A TEMPORARY CHAIRMAN may be elected to control a particular meeting. This may happen, for instance, if the CHAIRMAN is absent and the group has no VICE-CHAIRMAN. At the start of a group's existence, a temporary chairman may be appointed to oversee the ELECTION of the permanent chairman if there is more than one candidate. He cannot oversee his own election, so he should not be one of the candidates for the permanent post.

The SECRETARY of a group often acts as CONVENOR, and sends out the NOTICE and AGENDA, as well as the

MINUTES of the previous meeting. At the meeting itself, he will generally record the minutes. He should have available copies of the past minutes, rule books, etc., as well as any other facts and figures he may need to refer to in order to advise the CHAIRMAN. He may be asked to read out the notice of the meeting and the minutes. Company secretaries have certain legally defined duties which are mainly executive and clerical in nature.

The TREASURER is the person who deals with the group's finances. He may be asked to present a financial report to the meeting and would be expected to advise on any financial matters that arose.

The OFFICERS or OFFICIALS of a group are the named members who run the group; they almost always include a CHAIRMAN, a SECRETARY and a TREASURER. There may be other named officers such as a publicity officer, a social secretary or a membership secretary, depending on the nature of the group. The word 'honorary' is often used before individual titles or in the term 'honorary officers' to indicate that the posts are voluntary.

NOMINATIONS and ELECTIONS are needed to appoint the OFFICERS. Nominations need a PROPOSER and a SECONDER, and many groups have rules concerning re-election of officers and the length of time for which an officer may serve. Nominations are sometimes submitted by post, in advance of a meeting, but they may be made during the meeting itself. Similarly, the election or VOTING may be by post or at the meeting. It is normal for some background information about the candidates to be circulated with postal voting papers. Alternatively, at a meeting, the proposer may be asked to say a few words about why he thinks the candidate should be elected. The previous CHAIRMAN (or a TEMPORARY CHAIRMAN) presides over the elections which often form part of the ANNUAL GENERAL MEETING.

The MEMBERS of an organisation are those people who satisfy the criteria for membership defined by the organisation. Their membership entitles them to a VOTE at meetings.

A COOPTED MEMBER of a committee is a MEMBER of the organisation who is asked to join a committee on a temporary basis. This may be to fill a gap resulting from resignation or sickness, or to supply specialist help. Cooption does not survive the re-election of a committee, but the coopted member often stands for ELECTION in any case. Where a committee has a defined total number of members, a person can only be coopted to the committee to fill a gap. A coopted member will usually attend all of the meeting and have voting rights.

A CONSULTANT is someone recruited from outside the membership of the group because of his specialised knowledge. Consultants are usually appointed on a short-term basis and only attend the relevant parts of the meeting. They have no voting rights.

Types of meeting

A PUBLIC MEETING is one open to anyone who cares to attend, regardless of membership.

An ORDINARY GENERAL MEETING is one open to any MEMBER of the organisation in question. Members may also be able to bring guests along. The meeting may be devoted entirely to business, perhaps dealing with reports from committees or MOTIONS put by members, or there may be a short business meeting followed by some other event such as a talk by a guest speaker or a formalised debate. Decisions made by ordinary meetings are known as RESOLUTIONS.

An EXTRAORDINARY GENERAL MEETING (EGM) is called when there is urgent business to be dealt with, and this business cannot wait for the next ORDINARY MEETING. An EGM may be called, for example, to deal with the unexpected replacement of a senior OFFICIAL, or to wind up (dissolve) the organisation. There are usually rules concerning the period of NOTICE to be given and who should be notified. The AGENDA for an EGM would contain just the urgent business, and not other business as well.

An ANNUAL GENERAL MEETING (AGM), as its name suggests, is held yearly. All companies and registered charities must meet legal requirements concerning the length of time between AGMs and the NOTICE given of them. An AGM usually includes reports from the OFFICERS (individually or from the committee as a whole) and the ELECTION of new officers.

A COMMITTEE MEETING is a meeting of the OFFICERS plus other committee members of an organisation. Committees may also be set up to deal with certain aspects of an organisation's business which it is not appropriate for the whole membership to deal with. This may be because meetings of the whole membership are too large to deal efficiently with the business, or because the matters can only be decided by people with particular expertise or interests. A committee is responsible to the full membership of an organisation, and may well be asked to produce reports or RECOMMENDATIONS for the organisation as a whole. However, a committee generally appoints its own CHAIRMAN and defines its own rules for how its meetings are run. Because committees are made up of small groups of people – ideally the smallest number consistent with usefulness (usually between five and twenty people) – they are usually run on rather more informal lines than large business meetings. Committee members are likely to sit round a table, and would not usually stand to speak. The subjects to be discussed may not always be described as MOTIONS and, depending on the rules, motions may not have to be SECONDED. Committees should always define a QUORUM, so that decisions can only be taken by a representative part of the committee.

Committees can be of several types. EXECUTIVE COMMITTEES are those made up of the OFFICERS of the organisation (plus other committee members), and their role is to be responsible for the overall management of the organisation. Such committees are elected by the MEMBERS on annual or other defined periodic basis. STANDING COMMITTEES are those which are set up on a permanent basis to deal with a particular activity of the organisation. They are usually made up of people with special expertise in that field, and members are invited to join the committee. AD HOC COMMITTEES are similar to standing committees in many ways, being made up of people with particular expertise or interests. However, they are set up on a more temporary basis for a particular purpose, and are wound up or dissolved once this has been achieved. Most AD HOC committees produce a report on their subject to submit to the organisation. If the committee is unable to agree on all parts of the report they may also produce a minority report. JOINT COMMITTEES, are committees set up by two or more organisations to coordinate their activities. Such committees may be standing or AD HOC committees.

A SUBCOMMITTEE is a committee set up by another committee, to deal with some of the detailed work of the larger committee. A subcommittee may, for example, oversee a particular project where it is unnecessary for the full committee to be involved in all the detailed decisions. A subcommittee is normally small in size (from three people upwards), and its members need not be on the full committee, though it is usual for there to be some overlap. The subcommittee members have no right to attend the full committee meetings. A subcommittee may be set up on a standing or *ad hoc* basis, and the full committee normally appoints a person (who need not be the same person as the subcommittee chairman) to report back to the main committee.

The programme

NOTICE must be given to those concerned before a meeting. This may be done by making an announcement at the previous meeting, by displaying notices in the press and elsewhere, or by sending individual notices to all those who are entitled to attend. The notice should state the date, time and place of the meeting and should indicate the main purpose(s) of the meeting. It is often accompanied by the AGENDA which details the business to be conducted. There are legal requirements concerning the STATUTORY NOTICE that many organisations, in particular companies, must give before meetings. These define the period of notice that must be given (which often depends on the type of meeting), who must be notified, and in what way. Such statutory notices usually also contain details of voting by PROXY for members unable to attend.

The AGENDA is a résumé of the business to be conducted by the meeting. It is usually circulated in advance of the meeting by the SECRETARY, who compiles it in consultation with the CHAIRMAN. There is generally accepted order for items within an agenda which is listed below.

MINUTES OF THE PREVIOUS MEETING
MATTERS ARISING (from the minutes)
CORRESPONDENCE
REPORTS
Other major items of business (itemised individually)
ANY OTHER BUSINESS (AOB)
Date and place of next meeting

As the meeting usually deals with the items in the order they are listed, the major items of business should be listed in a logical order. However, at the chairman's discretion the order can be changed. Ideally, any such changes should be announced at the beginning of the meeting.

The MINUTES are a record of what happens at a meeting, and they are usually taken by the SECRETARY. They must obviously be accurate, and should be stored safely by the group so that they can, if necessary, be referred to at a future date. Individual minuted items should be numbered. Minutes are usually written in the same order as the AGENDA and would include the following details.

Title of meeting

Date and place where held, and time of start of meeting

Names and titles of officers present, plus names of other members present

Names of others present and reason for their presence (e.g. as an 'Observer')

(N.B. In a large meeting only the officers would be named and just the numbers of members and others present would be given)

Apologies for absence

An account of the formalities dealt with (e.g. 'The minutes of the previous meeting were read and signed by the chairman')

A summary of the discussions, decisions and actions required (for the main items of business)

The date (and place) of the next meeting

The time the meeting finished

In a formal meeting the summary of the main items of business must include the exact wording of the MOTIONS discussed, the names of the PROPOSER and SECONDER, and the results of the VOTING. To ensure the correct wording, proposers may often be asked to submit their motion in writing. The minutes should also mention any motions which were WITHDRAWN before voting. During the meeting, the chairman may ask that particular statements be minuted. Often the discussions and decisions resulting from them are written, down in chronological order, with an action column including the initials of the person or committee who should act upon the decision. The chairman should make sure that someone is made responsible to act on each decision made as necessary. However, other arrangements of minutes are possible, and some organisations like to list discussions, decisions, and actions separately. This has the advantage that it soon becomes obvious if the meeting is doing more discussing that decision-making!

The MINUTES OF THE PREVIOUS MEETING are one of the first items of business at any meeting. The minutes in question are those of the last meeting of the same type (i.e. the last AGM at an AGM, or the last ORDINARY MEETING at an ordinary meeting). The minutes may be read out by the SECRETARY, or if they have been circulated beforehand they are usually taken 'as read'. At this stage only their literal accuracy should be discussed, and once everyone is agreed that they are accurate, the minutes are signed by the CHAIRMAN.

'MATTERS ARISING' is the stage in the meeting when other questions relating to the MINUTES are discussed. For example, someone may question whether a certain letter mentioned on the previous minutes was written, and if so what reply has been received. Items specifically mentioned later in the AGENDA should not be brought up during 'Matters Arising'.

CORRESPONDENCE and REPORTS do not come up in all meetings. The correspondence that is mentioned should only be that relevant to the meeting, and it should be summarised by the SECRETARY, although he should have the actual letters available should anyone wish to see them.

'ANY OTHER BUSINESS' (AOB) is the stage at which members can bring up any other items of business not included in the main AGENDA. AOB should only include minor items, or business that has arisen too late to have been included as a main item in the agenda.

Control and procedure

A QUORUM is defined in the rules or constitutions of many organisations. It is a definition of the minimum number (or percentage) of people who must be present for the meeting to proceed. Quorum rules are designed to make sure that decisions are not taken by too small and unrepresentative a group of members, and the quorate number may be different for different types of meetings. For example, an EXTRAORDINARY GENERAL MEETING (which is likely to be discussing major policy) usually has a higher quorum than an ORDINARY MEETING. The CHAIRMAN should make sure the meeting is quorate before it starts. If the meeting is not quorate, but more members are expected, it may be possible to discuss some of the minor items of business. However, any decisions made must be ratified once the meeting is quorate.

POINTS OF ORDER may be made by anybody at a meeting if they notice some irregularity in procedure or behaviour which has not been spotted by the CHAIRMAN. For example, the person may point out that the meeting is not QUORATE, or that a person speaking is not entitled to do so at that point. Points of order can also be used if someone is being unjustifiably insulting or is disturbing the meeting in some way. A person may put a point of order at any time during the meeting and the chairman must consider it straightaway. If the chairman accepts the point, the irregularity must be dealt with immediately; if it is not accepted, the meeting proceeds as before.

POINTS OF INFORMATION can also be made at any time during a meeting, but they should only be used to ask a question or make a point directly connected with what the speaker is saying. For example, if someone quoted an incorrect figure, someone else may wish to interrupt with the correct one. The CHAIRMAN should ask the speaker if he is willing to accept a point of information (he is under no obligation to do so), and if so the question or point should be made and answered briefly before proceeding with the rest of the meeting.

In formal meetings, the points to be discussed are put as MOTIONS. If possible these should be sent to the SECRETARY beforehand, so that they can be included in the AGENDA. However, sometimes items that need decisions may only come up during a meeting, and someone may be asked to frame a motion there and then. So that the correct wording is discussed and recorded, motions should, wherever possible, be written down by their PROPOSER, and they should start with the word 'That'. For example, a motion might read, 'That—be done.' Motions normally need to have a PROPOSER and a SECONDER, and in formal meetings and debates there may be rulings as to the order in which people speak for or against the motion and whether they are allowed to speak more than once.

If someone supports the general ideas of a MOTION, but does not agree with all details, he may propose an AMENDMENT. Again, ideally, amendments should be proposed in time to be included in the AGENDA, but in practice this is seldom possible. In formal meetings, amendments are treated like motions and need a PROPOSER and a SECONDER and, after discussion, are put to the VOTE. If an amendment is accepted, the changes in question are made to the original motion, but if it is rejected the original motion remains (unless there are other amendments which are then each dealt with in the same way). The CHAIRMAN should make sure that amendments are not, in fact, alternative motions in disguise, and would not, for example, allow the insertion of the word 'not' which would simply reverse the meaning of the original motion.

Matters can get quite complicated, as it is possible to propose AMENDMENTS TO AMENDMENTS. However, in general the CHAIRMAN should work backwards, dealing with the smallest issues first (amendments to amendments) and working back towards the original MOTION. But, in the British Parliament the opposite course is taken and motions are voted on before amendments. Some political debates may follow this latter system, and if the motion is carried the amendment automatically fails.

The PROPOSER is the person who puts forward a MOTION or AMENDMENT. He should briefly explain what he has in mind, and should start and/or close his speech with the actual words of his motion.

The OPPOSER is the person who, in formal debates, puts the opposing view. He should be allowed as much time to speak as the PROPOSER.

The SECONDER is a person who announces that he is willing to support (or 'second') the MOTION or AMENDMENT put forward by the PROPOSER. If the rules of the organisation state that motions or amendments must be seconded, they automatically fail if no-one if found to second them.

During a debate, there are a number of procedures which can be followed which affect whether a VOTE is taken, whether all AMENDMENTS are discussed, and even whether the particular motion or the whole meeting is ADJOURNED or brought to a CLOSE. These procedures can get very complicated, and only the briefest of details are given below. Readers who want more details should refer to a book dealing specifically with formal business meetings.

ORDINARY CLOSURE involves the proposal of the motion, 'That the question now be put'. This can be used to bring lengthy discussion to a close. If the motion is accepted, the original MOTION under debate is briefly summed up by its PROPOSER and then put to the VOTE.

GUILLOTINE CLOSURE occurs when a motion, 'That the discussion on motion Z be limited to X hours and Y minutes' is passed. This guillotine motion would be taken before motion Z, and then motion Z would be voted on once the defined time is up, whatever, the state of the discussion.

KANGAROO CLOSURE is a method whereby the organisation votes to let the CHAIRMAN select which AMENDMENTS be discussed. Its success depends on the chairman making a wise selection, but it is a procedure which can save much time if there are numerous similar amendments.

LEAVE TO WITHDRAW a MOTION (or AMENDMENT) may be requested by the person who proposed the motion being discussed. If it is agreed, th discussion is terminated and no vote is taken on that motion. The PROPOSER may ask for this, for example, if he feels that his motion is unlikely to get sufficient support to be accepted, and wants to withdraw it in order to be able to resubmit it at some more favourable time. If others are against this leave being given, they can ask that the leave to withdraw be put to the VOTE.

The PREVIOUS QUESTION and the NEXT BUSINESS procedures are similar to LEAVE TO WITHDRAW to a motion, but are proposed by someone other than the PROPOSER of the original MOTION or AMENDMENT under discussion. If they are carried, the amendment or motion under discussion is not voted on, and the meeting returns to the original (previous) motion (question) or passes on to the next item (business).

It is possible to ADJOURN A DEBATE, perhaps to give people more time to think about the matter or get more information. If a MOTION is proposed that a discussion be adjourned, the motion should include details of when the discussion should resume – either later in the meeting, or in a future meeting.

Similarly, a motion to ADJOURN A MEETING should state when the remainder of the business of the meeting should be resumed. This may be later in the same day or in a meeting specially called to complete the business. A meeting may be adjourned because it has already taken up all the time available without completing business. Adjournment may also be suggested if tempers have become rather frayed, in order to allow people to calm down.

If a meeting is CLOSED by the chairman before all its business is complete, the additional items will only come up in the following meeting if they are specifically put forward as items for the next AGENDA.

Voting

As described in the previous section, not all MOTIONS and AMENDMENTS get put to the vote, and in an informal meeting the CHAIRMAN may just ask for the general assent of the group before a decision is recorded. He should always remind members of the wording of the motion before this decision is made. Even in a more formal meeting, if nearly everyone seems to share the same opinion he may just ask, 'Do I take it that you wish me to record this motion as passed (or rejected)?', but the members may demand that the motion be put to the vote.

The most informal type of vote is the SPOKEN VOTE, where the members simply say 'Aye' or 'No' depending on whether they support the motion or not. If the feeling of the meeting is obvious, this may be sufficient, but if there is any dispute a show of hands may be requested.

When voting is by a SHOW OF HANDS the chairman will ask those in favour, then those against the motion to raise their hands and, if necessary, the hands will be counted by tellers. He will also ask who wishes to abstain.

For important or closely contested issues, VOTING PAPERS may be issued to those eligible to vote.

A vote is only CARRIED UNANIMOUSLY if no eligible voter has abstained. If all those who voted are in favour, but some people have abstained, the result is known as NEM CON (none against).

Before a vote, anyone who is likely to benefit from the proposals put in a MOTION is expected to DECLARE AN INTEREST. He would then generally be expected to abstain from voting on the motion.

If the vote results in a draw, the CHAIRMAN may wish to use his CASTING VOTE. There is often confusion in organisations as to whether the chairman has a vote as an ordinary member plus a casting vote when there is a draw, or whether he is only entitled to vote in the event of a draw. The chairman does not have to use his casting vote, and he may decide that it is better to carry the motion forward to a future meeting, by which time people may have gravitated towards one view or the other.

In company and trade union meetings in particular, other specialised types of voting may be used. PROXY VOTING is where someone gives written permission for someone else to cast a vote on his behalf. It is commonly used in votes involving large numbers of shareholders. CARD or BLOCK VOTING, is often used by trade unions. In such a vote, delegates are entitled to vote on behalf of the number of members they represent. They often have cards with the number of votes they are entitled to cast, and these numbers are totalled up to give the overall result.

Sample Speeches

Thanking a speaker after a talk

Mr Chairman, Ladies and Gentlemen: Few people have not heard of the fabled Magic Carpet which could waft those sitting on it from one exotic place to the next, and spread before them fascinating panoramas of the world's wonders.

Tonight, after hearing about Mr X's travels in the Andes Mountains of Bolivia and Peru, I, for one, feel as if I've just stepped off that Magic Carpet. I'm sure it is the same for all of us.

However, there was something special about Mr X's talk. As we know, Peru and Bolivia hold tremendous interest for tourists and we would, of course, all love to go there. But Mr X did not just leave it at tourism. He has also made us aware of how people live in the Andes and what difficulties and hardships they have to face. It demonstrates Mr. X's sensitive approach to his subject that he not only records the marvels of Maccu Picchu – and how intriguing that ancient mountain city looked in his slides – but also photographed the people and the resigned look of hopeless poverty in so many of their faces. Mr X has done much more, therefore, than inform and entertain us, though he has done both brilliantly. He has opened our eyes to life and conditions in other countries where people are not so fortunate nor so secure as we are ourselves. Mr. X has given us an eye-opener as well as a very absorbing evening, and on behalf of all of us here, I would like to express to him our sincere thanks and appreciation.

Patriotic toast

Mr Chairman, Gentlemen: There are those about today who question whether a nation like ours needs to have armed forces. If, they say, we are really the peace-loving people we purport to be, why bother to equip an army, navy and air force? It is, of course, very naive to presume that the world is so calm a place that we may not need at some time to fight for the freedoms and principles we value. And though it may seem paradoxical, it is often necessary to fight for the peace which is precious to all of us.

This is why I feel honoured to propose this toast to Her Majesty's Forces, because those forces are not intended for making war, but for guarding the peace. Our own century and its many terrible conflicts have shown how much peace needs to be guarded – and also how skilfully and resolutely. If our nation is at peace today, and its citizens can lead their lives in a reasonable security, it is precisely because Her Majesty's Armed Forces have given, and continue to give this country, so great a measure of that skill and that resolution. Many, we know, have given the most any man or woman can give: they have lost their lives in the course of their duties. The peace preserved by our soldiers, sailors and airmen is not a gift – it has a price. I spoke of skill just now. Today, the profession of arms requires more skill than it ever did. Modern technology has seen to it that members of our armed forces must not only be disciplined and dedicated, but also reach high standards in many of the sciences. It is all the more to their credit that, because of their profession, they must be prepared to exercise their skills in situations where the lives of their comrades, and their own, may be at risk. To be a member of Her Majesty's Armed Forces is not just a job. The circumstances in which our forces operate bring valuable qualities to the fore, such as friendship, comradeship and courage. These are qualities which we all respect, and in which our soldiers, sailors and airmen have long set the rest of us a fine example to follow.

Gentlemen, I take pride in giving you the toast of Her Majesty's Forces.

Toast to 'Our Guests'

Mr Chairman, Ladies and Gentlemen: When I was asked to propose the toast to our guests this evening, a poem we all know came into my mind. However, if I quote from Coleridge's *The Ancient Mariner*, please don't get me wrong. I'm not going to compare our guests to the albatross which that unfortunate sailor had round his neck. Far from it – my quote is, 'The guests are met, the feast is set, may'st hear the merry din.'

We met our guests two or three hours ago. At that juncture, most of them were strangers to us, though of course we were very pleased that they should show enough interest in our club to give up an evening and spend it with us. We greatly appreciate, too, the fact that many of our guests have travelled a long way to be here tonight. Now, after only a short time in their company, I know I speak for all club members when I say that our guests have become new friends, and very generous ones, too. They have listened patiently while we told our old cricketing stories. They've admired our cups and our trophies. They've heard all about our hopes for next season. I, for one, admire their patience and fortitude and hope we haven't bored them too much, or indeed, at all. As for the feast being set, I'd like to turn that round and say that I think it was our guests who set the friendly and relaxed atmosphere for our feast. They certainly made us feel glad we invited them, and we've been congratulating ourselves on our choice of guests ever since we sat down to this dinner. After all, it's not easy to be a guest. Just think of the prospects: you probably don't know the people, the place, the menu – or the length of the after-dinner speeches you're going to have to sit through. However, our guests tonight took up the challenge in great spirits and if, to paraphrase Coleridge, the din- [pause] -ner was merry, it was very much due to their friendliness and good humour. It has been a pleasure to host a dinner with such guests. We've enjoyed your company. I hope you have enjoyed ours, and please come again. Ladies and Gentlemen, I give you the toast of: our guests.

Best man's speech at a wedding

Someone once wrote that the most precious possession that ever comes to a man is a woman's heart. Today, we've watched Bob attain his most precious possession by marrying Lucy, and we can see what a marvellous effect it's had on him. The chap's positively beaming, isn't he? And who can blame him? Lucy's a very lovely girl, and that heart of hers which she's given Bob today is a wonderfully kind and generous one. I know she's going to make him happy in the future, even happier than he is today, if that is possible.

But what, you may ask, is the most precious possession that ever comes to a woman? Well, I can honestly say that it's a fellow like Bob. Bob and I have known each other so long that I can't remember *not* knowing him. Since our old headmaster isn't here, it's safe to let you in on a state secret he and I have kept for years: we used to copy each other's homework at school – that's how well we know one another. I've always found Bob a good friend, not just when things are going right, but at other times, when they've not been so rosy. Bob has always been the sort of friend you could rely on absolutely, and not everyone can say they have that sort of pal in their lives.

Wedding days are meant to be unforgettable and this one certainly will be. I, for one, won't forget how heart-warming it was to see two super people like Bob and Lucy making their vows to each other this afternoon. I won't forget how great it has made me feel to be their best man. And I won't forget what a pleasure it is seeing them now, sharing the happiness of their great day with all of us, and the obvious joy all this has given their parents and families.

However, I must admit to a bit of disappointment. Lucy, as you know, has no sisters, just four brothers – and how she's survived to be as good natured as she is with that lot around, I really don't know. But it does mean that there aren't any more at home like her, so I'll just have to look elsewhere before I can claim my own most precious possession. I know I'll be very lucky indeed if I do half as well as Bob, but with his example before me, I'm certainly going to try.

Chairman's after-dinner speech at a charity function

[Charity supports home for Down's Syndrome sufferers]

Ladies and Gentlemen: It's a risky business organising a dinner like this, so you could say that, as organiser, I'm relieved as well as delighted to see you here. Some weeks ago, when you were blissfully unaware of what was going on, I was having a few nightmares. Would anybody want to come, I wondered. Surely they're sick of the sight of each other after working together all last year – daytimes, evenings *and* weekends – on our many fund-raising projects. Surely, thought I, they're sick of me, and the sound of my voice, after all the telephone calls I've made? I know I've interrupted your TV programmes too often, woken you up on weekend mornings and got many of you in from the garden on the few sunny days last summer afforded. I must say, I thought you might want your revenge. I did make a plan to have you frisked before you came in here, for eggs, tomatoes and anything else you might want to throw at me.

But you're a generous lot, in more ways than one, and I know you've put my intrusions down to the deep committment we all feel for the work we are doing. Your own personal committment has been nothing short of tremendous. The word 'success' could be stamped on everything you've undertaken this year. The dance was a success, so were the bring and buy sales, the coffee mornings the whist drives – everything. I'm glad to say we overshot our target, and have been able to do even more than we planned with the money you've raised. Cameron House now has three colour TVs instead of two, and the patients were able to spend a whole week, rather than the weekend originally planned, on their trip to France. There were four theatre visits last year instead of the two we thought we could manage, and we hired a bigger hall for the Christmas party and bought in more presents. So you really deserve to rest on your laurels, for this evening at least. Tomorrow, of course, the work begins again. The needs of those we're trying to help are never-ending, and our committment to it can never – must never – flag.

What is the nature of that committment? Most of us came to be working for Cameron House because we knew or had seen people suffering from Down's Syndrome. I always think of them that way because I find the term 'mongol' offensive. To identify human beings by their disability, be it mongol, leper or paraplegic, suggests that that is all they are. Even so, I'm sure we all remember our emotions at our first encounter – pity, maybe, thankfulness for our own good health and the health of our children, perhaps even a touch of guilt that we, the so-called 'normal ones', have been favoured when others have been so cruelly betrayed by Nature. And what about those fears we all felt? Would we react with disgust and make fools of ourselves or worse? Would we be patronising? Would we know how to talk to Down's sufferers or treat them like idiots? After all, it's not so long since the normal thing to do was to shut such people away, so that we didn't have to think about them, let alone meet them.

Having worked with this organisation for quite a few years now, I've become more and more convinced that we were missing a great deal by isolating Down's sufferers in that way. No-one pretends that Down's is not a great tragedy. But the wonderful thing is that the sufferers are not tragic. If anyone proves conclusively the ability of the human spirit to triumph over disaster, it's them. You can start talking to them and the back of your mind tells you that you must use simple words only, and speak slowly in case they can't hear you. Then, before you know where you are, you find your-self taken over by *their* personalities, *their* curiosity about *you*, *their* opinions about something you were going to make simple talk for them. It's a salutary experience we've all been through, and it quite upends preconceived notions.

I know I could be accused of speaking to the converted here, but it's no bad thing to take opportunities like this to express feelings which we all share. And I know we share the feeling that we aren't just helping a group of passive unfortunates. Because *they* help *us* by making us aware of something very positive that it's easy to overlook. Pick up a newspaper or switch on the television, and it's easy to despair of the world. But go to Cameron House and meet a

Down's sufferer and you realise how indestructible people can be, and how often a pleasant nature and good humour can't be defeated even by the worst disabilities.

I expect some of you know the story of John Merrick, the so-called Elephant Man, which was made into a film a while back. Merrick suffered from tumours which covered most of his body and deformed his head and face quite horribly. This was in the 1880s, and the only way Merrick could live was to exhibit himself as a fairground freak. I wonder how many of our friends at Cameron House would have suffered a similar fate had they lived a century ago? Merrick was lucky, though. He was rescued from the fairground by a young doctor called Frederick Treves who gave him a home at the London Hospital. Treves' sympathy had been triggered by the degrading and squalid life Merrick had been forced to lead, but at first his chief interest was purely professional. Treves wanted to examine Merrick and study him as an example of a strange, unknown medical condition. It wasn't long, though, before Treves discovered the personality behind the disability. This is what he wrote about Merrick:

'It would be reasonable to surmise that he would become a spiteful and malignant misanthrope, swollen with venom and filled with hatred of his fellow man, or on the other hand, that he would degenerate into a despairing melancholic. Merrick, however, was no such being. His troubles had ennobled him, he showed himself to be a gentle, affectionate and lovable person, free from any trace of cynicism or resentment . . .'

I feel that there are many similarities between the story of Treves and John Merrick and our relationships with our friends at Cameron House. And there's another important aspect to be mentioned here. Before I joined our organisation I used to think, like most people, that if I were paralysed, or blinded or damaged in some other dreadful way, I would come to hate and resent my fate, and quite probably not want to go on living. What Down's sufferers have taught me is not necessarily that while there's life, there's hope: maybe one day a cure for Down's will be found, but it's not here yet. No, what I've learned from them is more like what Treves learned from Merrick – that while there's life, there's *life* and some of the best things in life can be enjoyed in spite of great misfortune.

Ladies and Gentlemen, thank you for being here. Thank you for listening to my thoughts. Thank you for everything you've done in the past, and for your efforts in the future.

Presentation to someone retiring

Today Mr. Wilson – or 'Sir' to our younger employees but dear old Jack to many of us – is retiring after nearly forty years with this company. We are all here to wish him well, and make today one he will be happy to remember in the future. However, don't let's fool ourselves that Jack's retirement is just something that is happening to him. We are all going to be affected by the fact that he won't be in his office any more. Many of us who have come to rely on him won't be able to go to him for the advice and help he's given so generously over the years.

I've never really believed in the saying 'No-one is indispensible' because in many ways 'indispensible' is what Jack Wilson has been. He started here forty years ago as a young lad in the packing department and rose by sheer hard work and dedication to be a manager, then a section head and finally our chief executive. That sort of progress takes many qualities – ability, tenacity, patience, good humour – and it's those qualities we're all going to miss after Jack retires today.

But if there's one thing in particular that has always impressed me about Jack Wilson, it is this: he never forgot what it was like to be new and starting out at the bottom of the ladder. He's given the same courtesy and good humour to the humblest and youngest among us as he's given to those more senior. Jack has done well with this company, there's no doubt about that, but he's never got high and mighty because of it. There are many of us here today who can remember how a kindly word from Jack or a piece of his commonsense advice have made our jobs that much easier to do. Good relations with his staff have always been a strongpoint with Jack. I recall that when I came here, I walked into Jack's department on my first day, feeling a bit lost. I found, to my surprise and pleasure that Jack himself was waiting there to greet me, show me round and introduce me to everyone. No-one was more junior than I was on that day, yet the Head of Department, as Jack then was, had taken time and trouble just to make me feel welcome. I think that this is why those of us who have had the pleasure of working for and with Jack Wilson over the years have always been a tight-knit group and why most of the time anyway, we've all got on so well together.

We also admire Jack Wilson as a man of great resourcefulness and wide interests. As many of you know, he was instrumental in starting up this firm's sports and recreation club and he was the leading light behind the annual firm's outings we've all enjoyed so much in the past. I think I can say with confidence that no other company in this town has the sort of social facilities for its staff that our own possesses, but then no other firm has had Jack Wilson. Mind you, I must admit that some of us kicked and screamed a bit when he proposed we all go to an opera – and he didn't spare us either, it was one of the 'heavy' ones. But I, for one, said 'Yes' for Jack's sake and ended up being very glad that I did. I gained a new interest out of it, and actually went of my own accord to the next opera performance. You made quite a convert there, Jack!

It has not been easy, though, for us to choose our parting gift, because we wanted it to say so much on our behalf. However, we all hope it expresses the very high regard and affection we all have for you, Jack, and we wish you the happiest of times in your retirement.

Replying to a presentation

Ladies and Gentlemen: A retiree, like myself, once made the shortest reply speech on record. He received his presentation, said 'Thanks!' and sat down. Now, I know you won't let me get away with that. Besides, just 'Thanks' isn't enough, because for me, this is both a happy and a sad day. Sad because leaving this firm after so many years is no small matter. I won't be idle in my retirement, of course, but I can't pretend today isn't a bit of a wrench. Yet it's happy, too, because Fred Jones has said such flattering things about me, and because you've all given so much thought to choosing this beautiful — as a parting gift. I will value it both for itself and for what it means to me. Thank you all.

Sample Note Cards

For illustrated talk on 'stamp collecting'

1 Posts before intro. of modern postage stamps, + info. ref. first stamps

(1a) Private/royal posts, postal runners/mail coaches

Slide 1: Mail coach, 1830s

(1b) British PO losing money in 1830s − recipients [who paid postage] often refused to pay. Rowland Hill (Postmaster General) had solution . . .

Slide 2: Portrait, Rowland Hill

(1c) R. Hill promoter/designer of first PRE-PAID stamp, Penny Black. Life/Work/Penny Black design [1840]

Slide 3: Penny Black, 1840

2 Spread of pre-paid postage/start of stamp collecting

(2a) New stamps issued by Switzerland, Spain, Brazil

Slide 4: First foreign stamps

(2b) Stamp collecting started 1841. At first, stamps stuck on walls, furniture − even chamber pots!

Slide 5: Room decorated in stamps [19th century]

119

(2c) Great/rich collectors in early days: mention Ferrary [spent £2,000 a week on stamps], Alfred Hind [burned valuable stamp to increase price of his own copy]. Other anecdotes

Slide 6: Portrait of Ferrary [dressed like tramp as he always did]

3 Collecting stamps

(3a) Why collect stamps? – for their beauty, educational value, subject interest, etc

Slide 7: Chinese stamps demonstrating all three reasons

(3b) Collecting by theme – reflects other interests viz. animals, aircraft, sports, etc

Slide 8: Selection of thematic stamps

(3c) Collecting by country – reasons: relatives abroad/visited country, now collects its stamps/just like the stamps!

Slide 9: My collection of France – two pages [tell my reasons for liking France]

4 How to obtain stamps, etc

(4a) Local stamp shop – what it contains, how it is arranged

Slide 10: Inside of stamp shop

(4b) Obtain stamps by mail order/ or by approval

Slide 11: Two page-spread from adverts in stamp mag

(4c) Stamps fairs/exhibitions

Slide 12: Local stamp fair scene

LAST WORD: Stress enjoyment in stamps and collecting

Chairman's report to a tennis club

1 Club thriving, very good year last year. Can be proud of ourselves

(1a) Financial situation/profit [healthy – everyone paid their subs.!]

(1b) New members who have joined in the last year – welcome

(1c) New facilities – new indoor tennis courts [weather-proof!] Club coach available four times per week, instead of three. New club minibus, etc

2 Future plans [exciting]

(2a) Inter-club contests – club teams to be faced in coming year. Their success record – must keep on our toes

(2b) Tennis weekend arranged for May – give brief details – outline benefits to club members – we expect big demand, so book early

(2c) Dates of professional tennis tournaments viz. Wimbledon, Queen's, Wembley – TV coverage abroad for Grand Slam events. Hopes for being lucky in draw for finals day, Wimbledon. Events Secretary can give details of group tickets for other tournaments

Talk at Public meeting [Subject: Proposed new major road through village

1 Village today and [if road goes through] tomorrow

(1a) *Our* village is beautiful/historic. Outline major history/past residents. Visitors come to see village – it's a tourist spot, but not spoiled by that

(1b) New road will alter village for the worse/disturb way of life/means dangers of many sorts

(1c) Dangers: noise/dirt/traffic jams/health hazards/risk of accidents/vibration damage to buildings from lorries/fumes/lead pollution

2 Why we should oppose new road

(2a) Not being obstinate/reactionary – want to preserve beauty/interest of village – things worth preserving, even fighting and arguing for

(2b) Viable alternatives: (a) widen existing major road/ (b) ring road (c) site road 10 miles north, where it will not disturb this or other villages in our area

(2c) Protest meetings like this not enough – must have campaign – use local press/local radio/lobby Parliament/ protest march [invite TV]

Index

Opening
doors to
the World
of books

Book Tokens

Book Tokens
can be
bought and
exchanged
at most
bookshops